M_{ATLAB}®
Tools
for Control System
Analysis
and Design

MATLAB®
Tools
for Control System
Analysis
and Design

Benjamin C. Kuo

Professor Emeritus
Department of Electrical and Computer Engineering
University of Illinois at Urbana-Champaign

Duane C. Hanselman

Associate Professor
Department of Electrical and Computer Engineering
University of Maine

The MATLAB® Curriculum Series

PRENTICE HALL Englewood Cliffs, NJ 07632

Library of Congress Cataloging-in-Publication Data

Kuo, Benjamin C.
    MATLAB tools for control system analysis and design / Benjamin C.
Kuo, Duane C. Hanselman.
        p.   cm. -- (MATLAB curriculum series)
    "For MS-DOS personal computers"--Cover.
    Includes bibliographical references and index.
    ISBN 0-13-034646-2
    1. Feedback control systems. 2. MATLAB. 3. MS-DOS (Computer
file)   I. Hanselman, Duane C. II. Title. III. Series.
TJ216.K816 1994
629.8'3--dc20   93-13935
                                                                 CIP

Acquisitions Editor: Don Fowley
Production Editor: Joe Scordato
Copy Editor: Andrea Hammer
Chapter Opener and Cover Designer: Jeanette Jacobs
Buyer: Dave Dickey
Editorial Assistant: Jennifer Klein

 © 1994 by Prentice-Hall, Inc.
A Paramount Communications Company
Englewood Cliffs, New Jersey 07632

Printed in the United States of America

10 9 8 7 6 5 4 3 2 1

ISBN 0-13-034646-2

Prentice-Hall International (UK) Limited, *London*
Prentice-Hall of Australia Pty. Limited, *Sydney*
Prentice-Hall Canada Inc., *Toronto*
Prentice-Hall Hispanoamericana, S.A., *Mexico*
Prentice-Hall of India Private Limited, *New Delhi*
Prentice-Hall of Japan, Inc., *Tokyo*
Simon & Schuster Asia Pte. Ltd., *Singapore*
Editora Prentice-Hall do Brasil, Ltda., *Rio de Janeiro*

Contents

———————————————————

*M*ATLAB®
Tools
for Control System
Analysis
and Design

Part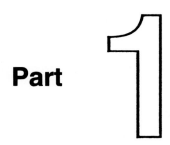

Getting Started

1

Jump Start—For Those Who Are in a Hurry!

Briefly, here is what you need to do to get going.

1. Create a place for the *CSAD Toolbox* to reside on your hard disk. On an MS-DOS PC this means creating a subdirectory named `CSAD` in the `MATLAB` subdirectory. On a Macintosh this means creating a folder named `CSAD_Toolbox` within the `MATLAB` folder.

2. Copy the files from the floppy disk into the subdirectory or folder you just made.

3. Make MATLAB aware of the new files so you can use them. On an MS-DOS PC this means adding the subdirectory `CSAD` to the `MATLABPATH`. On a Macintosh this means throwing out the `MATLAB Settings` file.

4. Initialize the software. To the MATLAB prompt type `>>csad <CR>`. (Note: you must do this once every time you start MATLAB and wish to use the *CSAD Toolbox*.) Then type `>>help csad <CR>` to see the names and a description of the most important functions in the *CSAD Toolbox*.

2

To the Instructor and Student

You're probably wondering why produce yet another software package for control system analysis and design? After all, many undergraduate texts in this area offer software packages to accompany the text material. Moreover, for those having *The Student Edition of MATLAB* or access to the professional version of MATLAB with the *Control System Toolbox*, this text and software may appear redundant.

So why another software package? The reason is to provide a set of tools that offers a consistent, convenient, and productive approach specifically focused at undergraduate control system analysis and design. By using MATLAB as the platform for the software, all the benefits of MATLAB can be utilized. For example, the underlying numerical algorithms in MATLAB are the best available, and MATLAB runs on all popular computers and on just about any monitor.

The Student Edition of MATLAB and the *Control System Toolbox* both offer many powerful tools (M-files) for the analysis of control systems. These tools were developed for users who are more familiar with control systems and with MATLAB than is the typical undergraduate student, who is learning the material for the first time. To address this issue, *MATLAB Tools for Control System Analysis and Design* offers a set of tools that minimizes the amount of MATLAB knowledge required. In doing so, the user can focus more clearly on thinking about and solving the control system problems at hand. Key to providing this focus is the inclusion of many menu-driven, user-interactive tools (i.e., function M-files). These tools offer menu options that allow the user to explore all topics of academic interest. Menu items include: finding the rise time, settling time, and percent overshoot from a step response plot; finding asymptote angles, angles of departure and arrival, and marginal stability points on a root locus plot; finding the peak resonance, bandwidth, and stability margins from a frequency response plot. In addition, specific menu-driven tools are provided for the design of PID and lead/lag controllers.

Finally, this text and software don't try to be everything for everyone. All control system analysis and design programs, including this one, have their own advantages as well as disadvantages. There are many things that are not done here, and certainly there are things that are done that you would like to see done differently. As a result, we would like to encourage you to provide feedback about those features you would like to see changed or added in future editions of this text and software. To do so, contact us at the address given below or better yet send E-mail or a FAX. Without your input, this is an open loop system. So take the time to close the loop. Your feedback is guaranteed to maintain stability and improve performance!

CSAD Toolbox
c/o Dr. Duane Hanselman
University of Maine
113 Barrows Hall
Orono, ME 04469

E-mail: CSAD@watson.eece.maine.edu
FAX: (207)-581-2220

3

About This Text

3.1 CONVENTIONS USED IN THIS TEXT

The following conventions are used throughout this text:

Bold Initial Caps   Key names, MATLAB menu names, MATLAB menu item names.

`Constant Width`   User input, function and file names, commands, and screen displays. Note: MATLAB commands are case sensitive, `<CR>` means pressing the return or enter key, and `>>` is the MATLAB prompt.

Italics   Book titles, names of sections of this text, important terms and concepts, MATLAB and toolbox names, and mathematical notation.

3.2 ORGANIZATION

This book is organized into three parts, each containing one or more chapters. The material you are reading now is Part 1: Getting Started. Part 2: Theory and Tools introduces important control system concepts and, more important, illustrates problem solving using *CSAD Toolbox* functions. In Part 3: *CSAD Toolbox* Reference, *CSAD Toolbox* functions are described in detail.

6

Hardware and Software

4.1 HARDWARE AND SOFTWARE REQUIREMENTS

The software provided with this text consists of a set of MATLAB M-files called the *Control Systems Analysis and Design Toolbox*, or *CSAD Toolbox*. These M-files will run on any computer that runs MATLAB and on any version 3.0 or later of the MATLAB software. The software has not been tested on version 4, so some minor problems may exist. To run well, the MATLAB workspace should have at least 100K bytes of available workspace. For most users, this should not pose a problem.

The *CSAD Toolbox* requires approximately 100K bytes of disk space depending upon the disk sector size. In addition, on MS-DOS computers, the operating system environment parameter space must be large enough to add the *CSAD Toolbox* to the parameter `MATLABPATH`. This will be more thoroughly discussed in the following installation chapter.

It is assumed that MATLAB and the *CSAD Toolbox* will be installed on a hard disk. With much reduced capabilities, MATLAB and the *CSAD Toolbox* can be installed on floppy disks.

See *The Student Edition of MATLAB* or the *MATLAB User's Guide* for further information on MATLAB requirements.

4.2 SOFTWARE INSTALLATION

The *CSAD Toolbox* is copyrighted and licensed for use on a single computer only. You are not allowed to give the program to friends or to install the software on multiple computers. **You are violating the law if you violate the license or copyright restrictions. Doing so makes you liable for criminal prosecution.**

We, the authors of this text, know how prevalent software piracy is, especially on college campuses where the desire for software often exceeds the resources to purchase it legally. Despite this, we encourage you to act responsibly and to encourage responsible actions by others. We are not a big faceless corporation that makes billions or even millions of dollars. Quite the contrary, we are two entrepreneurs who have spent many hours in the hopes of providing quality software at a very reasonable price. So, before you engage in or promote the piracy of this software ask yourself the question: Would I do this if I were the author of this work?

4.2.1 MS-DOS Personal Computers (PCs)

The *CSAD Toolbox* is distributed on one 720K byte 3.5″ diskette or one 360K byte 5.25″ diskette. The procedure described subsequently creates a subdirectory for the *CSAD Toolbox*, copies the M-files to that subdirectory, and modifies the MATLABPATH so that MATLAB recognizes the M-files in the *CSAD Toolbox*.

The following instructions assume that drive A is a floppy disk drive and drive C is the hard disk where the software is to be installed. If this is not the case, substitute the appropriate drive designations, or seek assistance from a more experienced PC user. All commands given are MS-DOS commands.

Procedure:

1. Create a subdirectory on the hard disk within the subdirectory where MATLAB resides (assumed to be c:\MATLAB), and set it to be the current directory.

    ```
    c> md \MATLAB\CSAD <CR>
    c> cd \MATLAB\CSAD <CR>
    ```

2. Insert the *CSAD Toolbox* diskette in drive A and type

    ```
    c> copy A:CSAD <CR>
    ```

3. Update the MATLAB search path. MATLAB's search path is specified in the environment parameter MATLABPATH. Somewhere on your system in a batch file (AUTOEXEC.BAT or MATLAB.BAT are likely possibilities) is a statement defining MATLABPATH. For example it could be

    ```
    set MATLABPATH=\MATLAB\MATLAB;\MATLAB\DEMO
    ```

The *CSAD Toolbox* location must be appended to this statement so that MATLAB can find the *CSAD Toolbox* M-files. Doing so to the preceding path statement gives

```
set MATLABPATH=\MATLAB\MATLAB;\MATLAB\DEMO;\MATLAB\CSAD
```

See *The Student Edition of* MATLAB or the MATLAB *User's Guide* for further information about MATLABPATH.

4.2.2 Macintosh Computers

The *CSAD Toolbox* is distributed on one 800K byte 3.5″ diskette. The procedure described subsequently creates a folder for the *CSAD Toolbox*, copies the M-files to that folder, and instructs you how to make MATLAB recognize the M-files in the *CSAD Toolbox*.

Procedure:

1. Open the folder where MATLAB resides so that you can see the MATLAB executable file and any currently available toolbox folders.
2. Insert the *CSAD Toolbox* diskette into an available disk drive, and open the disk so that the CSAD_Toolbox folder appears.
3. Drag the CSAD_Toolbox folder to the open window where the MATLAB executable file resides.

Normally, MATLAB on the Macintosh should find the M-files in the CSAD_Toolbox folder. To make sure that it does, throw out the file named MATLAB Settings before you start MATLAB. Doing so makes MATLAB create a new settings file that includes the CSAD_Toolbox folder.

See *The Student Edition of* MATLAB or the MATLAB *User's Guide* for further information.

4.3 HARDCOPY OUTPUT

Numerical and graphics hardcopies can be obtained in several ways in MATLAB while using the *CSAD Toolbox* functions. On MS-DOS computers, the procedures are more involved than on Macintosh computers.

4.3.1 MS-DOS PCs

The easiest way to obtain numerical and graphical hardcopies from an MS-DOS PC is through the normal PC screen dump technique of pressing the **Shift-PrtSc** keys. Although this always works for the MATLAB command screen that contains alphanumerical data. screen dumps from MATLAB graphics screen only work if you have loaded the appropriate graphics driver.

MS-DOS comes with several drivers for specific monitors and printers. In addition, *The Student Edition of MATLAB* and *Professional MATLAB* both come with drivers that are configured for EGA/VGA monitors dumping to Epson or HP Laserjet printers. The appropriate driver is normally run during system startup as one command in the `AUTOEXEC.BAT` file.

For those running *Professional MATLAB*, it is possible to use the available metafile and graphics postprocessor capabilities. Within the menu-driven *CSAD Toolbox* functions these features can be accessed through the ! menu option. See the reference section for further information about the ! menu option.

Further information on MS-DOS PC hardcopy is available by consulting *The Student Edition of MATLAB* or the *MATLAB User's Guide*.

4.3.2 Macintosh Computers

Hardcopy on the Macintosh follows the traditional Macintosh intuitive approach. Information from the command screen can be printed by highlighting the desired text with the mouse, then choosing **Print** from the **File** menu. If no text is highlighted, the entire command window is printed. In a similar fashion, choosing **Print** from the **File** menu with the graphics screen active sends the current graph to the printer.

The Macintosh clipboard feature also works in MATLAB. Thus, highlighted portions of the command screen and the graphics screen can be copied to the clipboard at any time for transfer to the scrapbook or another program.

Further information on Macintosh hardcopy is available by consulting *The Student Edition of MATLAB* or the *MATLAB User's Guide*.

5

About the CSAD Toolbox

5.1 INITIALIZING THE *CSAD TOOLBOX*

Before it is possible to use any of the *CSAD Toolbox* functions, it is necessary to type CSAD to the MATLAB prompt:

```
>>csad <CR>
```

This M-file displays the current software version number and other important information. After reviewing the displayed information, the remaining *CSAD Toolbox* functions are enabled. Note that this must be done once in every MATLAB session where the *CSAD Toolbox* is used.

5.2 ASSUMPTIONS

5.2.1 MATLAB Familiarity

This text and software assumes that you have at least some idea about what to do when faced with the MATLAB prompt >>. For example, you should know what happens when you type:

```
>>a=10*[1 2 3]';<CR>
>>b=a.^2; <CR>
>>c=b-a; <CR>
>>d=log(c); <CR>
```

You should know how MATLAB represents polynomials. That is, to MATLAB a polynomial is a row vector of its coefficients in descending order. Thus,

```
>>n=[1 2 3 0] <CR>
```

is the polynomial $n(s) = s^3 + 2s^2 + 3s + 0$. More will be said about polynomials in Sections 5.4 and 5.5.

Though it is not absolutely necessary, it is helpful if you are somewhat familiar with common MATLAB functions such as:

```
>>theta=linspace(0,2*pi); <CR>
>>x=sin(theta); <CR>
>>y=cos(theta); <CR>
>>z=2*x.*y; <CR>
```

and can generate simple plots such as:

```
>>plot(theta,x,theta,y,theta,z) <CR>
```

The following is a short list of MATLAB functions you may wish to become familiar with by consulting *The Student Edition of* MATLAB or the MATLAB *User's Guide*:

```
+, -, *, /, \, ', ^        real, imag, conj
.*, ./, .\, .', .^         exp, log, log10,
help                       sin, cos, tan
who, whos, what, dir       poly, roots, eig
^C (or) ⌘                  rank, det, inv
pi, sqrt(-1), inf          eye, ones, zeros
hold, grid                 linspace, logspace
ginput, gtext              abs, sqrt
format, diary              plot, title, text
```

5.2.2 Control Systems Familiarity

The primary purpose of this text is to supplement typical junior- and senior-level undergraduate control systems texts. As a result, it is assumed that you are taking a control systems course at this time or have taken one in the past. The material presented here is neither rigorous nor complete. Its sole purpose is to describe the features found in the *CSAD Toolbox*.

Specifically, it is assumed that you are familiar with the Laplace transform and sinusoidal steady-state analysis. You should know what a Bode plot is. The concept of an *s*-plane, and poles and zeros should be familiar to you. The transfer function description of a system should be understood. It is not necessary to understand fully the state-variable description of a system.

5.3 RESTRICTIONS

5.3.1 Single-Input, Single-Output Systems

The *CSAD Toolbox* functions were written to handle systems having a single input and a single output (SISO). It is possible to perform some multiple-input, multiple-output (MIMO) system analysis by considering a single input-output pair at a time.

The reason for considering only SISO systems is twofold. First, many control systems are SISO, and a thorough understanding of SISO concepts is required before MIMO system analysis can be conducted. And, second, the syntax burden of carrying around input and output terminal designations would make the software more cumbersome and less intuitive than it is for SISO systems.

5.3.2 Numerical Accuracy

As good as MATLAB is, it still suffers from the fact that computers cannot represent all numbers with infinite precision. In addition, because computers cannot evaluate functions at an infinite number of points, we are forced to accept samples of a function evaluated at a finite number of points. These two facts can lead to erroneous results or to an erroneous interpretation of the results produced by MATLAB and the *CSAD Toolbox* functions. To minimize the possibility of this occurring

1. Keep your system order low. Numerical accuracy decreases as system order increases. This can be accomplished by eliminating nondominant or parasitic system poles. In general, the closer all the poles of a system are together, the more accurate results will be.

2. Avoid calculations that involve the inverse of matrices that are singular or nearly so. An example of this is trying to find the transformation matrix that converts a system to controllable (or observable) canonical form when the system is uncontrollable (or unobservable). Another example is trying to find the state feedback gains for a system that is nearly uncontrollable.

3. MATLAB plots are constructed by connecting data points together with straight lines. As a result, plots that are magnified by using the `Zoom in` feature found in many *CSAD Toolbox* functions can look rough because only a few data points remain to compose the entire plot.

4. The accuracy of calculations based on plotted data such as step response attributes (`attributes` in the functions `tftplot` and `svplot`) and

frequency-domain specifications (`margins` in the functions `bplot`, `mvpplot`, and `plrplot`) is dependent on the resolution of the underlying data. The *CSAD Toolbox* functions were written with the compromise between speed and accuracy in mind. Generally, the results should exhibit errors no greater than 1%, although under some circumstances it is possible to see much larger errors.

5.4 USER INPUT

Many of the *CSAD Toolbox* functions prompt the user for input. These prompts are of seven different types: yes/no, single number, character string, polynomial, vector, matrix, and graphical. In the following, each of these prompts is discussed.

5.4.1 Yes/No Input

An example of a yes/no prompt is

```
Label K on graph? (y/n) [n] >
```

This prompt appears in the *CSAD Toolbox* M-file `rlplot`. The term (`y/n`) indicates that a `y`(es) or `n`(o) answer is requested. The term [`n`] indicates the default input of `no` is assumed if only the return key (<CR>) is pressed. Sometimes no default input is displayed, in which case a `y` or `n` must be entered. At other times a [`y`] default input is displayed. In all cases, uppercase or lowercase characters may be entered.

5.4.2 Single-Number Input

An example of a single-number prompt is

```
Enter START frequency, w = 10^k1, k1 = [-1.000] >
```

This prompt is in the *CSAD Toolbox* M-file `bplot`. Here [`-1.000`] indicates the default value given to `k1`, the power of 10 marking the start frequency of a Bode plot. As before, the default value may or may not appear. If it does not, a number must be entered. The input to a single-number prompt can be any valid MATLAB statement that produces a single number. Examples include `1/3`, `-1`, `sqrt(2)`, `4*atan(1)`, `10+sqrt(-1)*tan(pi/3)`. When a vector or matrix-valued input is entered only the first element is accepted.

When the default input is given, it is possible to use its value as part of your response. For example, given the prompt:

```
Enter desired final time [2.35] >
```

The default final time is the current final time of 2.35 s. If you wish to cut the final time to 60% of its current value, you can enter `1.41` or `0.6*def`, where the variable `def` is the default value.

5.4.3 Character String Input

An example of a character string prompt is

```
Enter title for plot:
```

No default input is given in character string prompts. User input is assumed to be a valid MATLAB string *without a beginning and ending quote*. Entering terminating quotes or noncharacter input will likely cause a MATLAB syntax error terminating the M-file in use.

5.4.4 Polynomial Input

An example of a polynomial prompt is

```
Default input is: s^2 + 10.00s^1 + 100.0
Enter Denominator polynomial >
```

Here the optional default input appears above the prompt. If the return key is pressed, the denominator polynomial is set to the default value. Even though the default polynomial is shown as a polynomial in `s`, the input requested must be in the form of a row vector of the desired polynomial coefficients. For example, the preceding default input could be reentered by typing `[1 10 100]` at the prompt.

Zero terms within a polynomial must be included. For example, the polynomial $s^2 + 10s$ is entered as `[1 10 0]`. The first term in a polynomial must be nonzero. Thus, even though $s^2 + 10s = 0s^3 + s^2 + 10s$, this polynomial cannot be entered as `[0 1 10 0]`.

When a default input is displayed, it is possible to use it to compose a new input. For example, suppose the prompt shown previously is displayed, and the desired input is simply five times the default polynomial. Then, the new input is entered as `5*def` where `def` is the default polynomial.

This feature is even more powerful when the desired input is the default input multiplied or added to another polynomial. For example, suppose the preceding prompt is displayed and the desired input is $(s^2 + 10s + 100)(s + 5)$. This input is entered as `pmult(def,[1 5])`, where `pmult` is a *CSAD Toolbox* function for multiplying polynomials.

Any valid MATLAB statement leading to a row vector is acceptable as input. Invalid input will likely cause a MATLAB syntax error terminating the M-file in use. See *Polynomial Manipulation* below for more information regarding polynomials in MATLAB.

5.4.5 Vector Input

An example of a vector prompt is

```
Enter K values to plot >
```

This prompt appears in the *CSAD Toolbox* M-file `rlplot`. For vector prompts, no default input is displayed even though one may exist. The existence of a default input should be apparent from the context of the prompt. If nothing is entered and no default input exists, the prompt will be repeated until you enter something. Any valid MATLAB statement leading to a vector is acceptable as input. Invalid input will likely cause a MATLAB syntax error terminating the M-file in use.

5.4.6 Matrix Input

A prompt for matrix input appears in *CSAD Toolbox* functions that use the state variable system description. An example of a matrix prompt is

```
A =
```

This prompt appears in the *CSAD Toolbox* M-file `svstuff`. It requests input for the A matrix of a system. Any valid MATLAB statement leading to a matrix is acceptable as input. Invalid input will likely cause a MATLAB syntax error terminating the M-file in use.

5.4.7 Graphical Input

In several *CSAD Toolbox* functions, you are prompted to identify one or more points on the graphics screen. An example that appears in a number of functions in response to the `Zoom in` menu choice is

```
Pick Lower Left and Upper Right corners for new plot
using the mouse and mouse button.
Press any key to continue. . .
```

If you have an installed mouse, press any key to make the graphics screen active. Then, for the preceding example, point the mouse pointer at the desired lower-left corner, and press any mouse button. Then do the same for the upper-right corner.

If you do not have an installed mouse, a crosshair will appear on the graphics screen instead of the mouse pointer. In this case move the crosshair with the cursor keys on your keyboard and press the **spacebar** to identify the desired point on the graph. Do *not* press the return or enter keys as this will likely cause a MATLAB syntax error terminating the M-file in use. Note that the resolution of the crosshair is poor relative to the mouse pointer, so it is more difficult to be precise using the cursor keys.

This completes the discussion of user prompts appearing in the *CSAD Toolbox* functions. For assistance in writing valid MATLAB statements leading to proper input see *The Student Edition of MATLAB* or the *MATLAB User's Guide*.

5.5 POLYNOMIAL MANIPULATION

In MATLAB polynomials are represented by row vectors of their coefficients in descending order. Thus, $3s^4 + 6s^3 + 2s^2 + 10$ is [3 6 2 0 10] in MATLAB. Because MATLAB cannot tell the difference between a row vector of numbers and a row vector representing a polynomial, manipulation of polynomials in MATLAB requires special treatment. The functions `pmult, padd, pmake` in the *CSAD Toolbox* and the standard MATLAB function `poly` provide this special treatment. `pmult` is a function that multiplies up to 10 polynomials. `padd` is a function that adds up to 10 polynomials. `pmake` constructs real polynomials given its roots. And `poly` is a function that creates any polynomial given its roots.

These four functions are very useful for providing input to *CSAD Toolbox* functions and to polynomial prompts within them. To illustrate these functions, consider the following examples:

Example 1:

$10s(s + 2)(s + 10)$ can be input as   `10*poly([0; -2; -10])`
                 or as   `10*pmake(0, -2, -10)`
                 or as   `10*pmult([1 0], [1 2], [1 10])`

In the first case, `poly` is used to create a polynomial having 0, −2, and −10 as its roots. (Note that polynomials in MATLAB are **row** vectors, and polynomial roots are **column** vectors, thus the reason for the semicolons making [0; -2; -10] a column vector. In the second case given previously, `pmake` is used to create the polynomial. In the third case, `pmult` is used to multiply the individual polynomial terms together. Obviously, there are also other ways to enter this polynomial.

Example 2:

$(4s^2 + 9s + 24) (s + 3) + (s + 2) (s + 10)$ can be input as

`padd(pmult([4 9 24], [1 3],poly([-2; -10]))`

Here `padd` is used to add the two pieces together after they are constructed using `pmult` and `poly`.

Example 3:

$(s + 1 + j2)(s + 1 - j2)(s + 3)$ can be input as

```
        poly([-1+sqrt(-1)*2;-1-sqrt(-1)*2;-3])
or as   poly([ccp(-1,2);-3])
or as   pmake(-1+sqrt(-1)*2,-3)
or as   pmake(ccp(-1,2),-3)
```

In this example a polynomial having complex roots is considered. The first case uses the function `poly` directly. In the second case, the *CSAD Toolbox* utility function `ccp` is called to generate the required complex conjugate pair for `poly`. The third case uses the *CSAD Toolbox* function `pmake` to form the polynomial. The last case calls the function `ccp` to form the required complex conjugate pair for `pmake`.

From the preceding it appears that `pmake` simply duplicates the capabilities of the built-in MATLAB command `poly`. Other than being able to enter roots as separate input arguments, `pmake` differs from `poly` in that `pmake` will always return a polynomial with real coefficients. Because `poly` is meant to work with complex polynomials also, `poly` sometimes will return a polynomial with residual imaginary coefficients because of numerical roundoff when multiplying complex conjugate roots.

For those familiar with MATLAB, `pmult` appears to duplicate the operation of the standard MATLAB function `conv`. This is true. However, `conv` is limited to multiplying 2 polynomials together, whereas `pmult` will multiply up to 10. The function `conv` is not introduced here because `pmult` is more general and perhaps easier to remember.

See *The Student Edition of MATLAB* or the *MATLAB User's Guide* for more information on `poly`. See the reference section of this text for more information on `ccp`, `pmult`, `padd`, and `pmake`.

Part 2

Theory and Tools

Mathematical Foundation

6.1 INTRODUCTION

The study of control systems rely heavily on mathematical tools that include *complex variable theory*, *differential equations*, *Laplace transformation*, and so on. These mathematical tools form the basic foundation for theoretical and analytical analysis and design of control systems. Computer-aided analysis and design tools such as MATLAB also depend heavily on the establishment of these mathematical tools.

In this chapter, we present the background material that is needed for the applications of the functions in the *CSAD Toolbox*. Much of the details of the necessary mathematical background can be found in standard texts on control systems and thus are not elaborated on here. In particular, the manual of *The Student Edition of MATLAB* covers matrix algebra extensively, and the subject is not duplicated here.

6.2 COMPLEX VARIABLES AND FUNCTIONS

6.2.1 Complex Variables

Classical control-system analysis and design relies heavily on the use of complex variables and their functions. By its design, MATLAB treats complex numbers routinely.

A complex variable s has two components: a real component σ and an imaginary component ω. Analytically, a complex number of variable is represented as

$$s = \sigma + j\omega \qquad (6\text{-}1)$$

which can be portrayed graphically in the two-axis coordinates, called the s-plane, as shown in Fig. 6-1. The powerful root locus diagram in control system analysis and design is done in the complex s-plane.

MATLAB displays a complex number as $\sigma + \omega i$, where σ and ω are real numbers. This notation conforms with conventional mathematical analysis, whereas the notation of $\sigma + j\omega$ conforms to conventional engineering analysis.

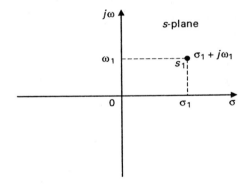

Figure 6-1. The complex s-plane.

6.2.2 Functions of a Complex Variable

Control systems analysis relies on the use of transfer functions that are functions of the complex variable s. The function $G(s)$ is said to be a single-valued function of the complex variable s if for every value of s, there is only one corresponding value of $G(s)$. Because s has real and imaginary parts, the function $G(s)$ also has real and imaginary parts; that is,

$$G(s) = \text{Re}[G(s)] + j\text{Im}[G(s)] \qquad (6\text{-}2)$$

where $\text{Re}[G(s)]$ denotes the real part of $G(s)$, and $\text{Im}[G(s)]$ denotes the imaginary part of $G(s)$. Thus, the function $G(s)$ is also represented graphically by the complex $G(s)$-plane, whose horizontal axis represents $\text{Re}[G(s)]$ and the vertical axis represents $\text{Im}[G(s)]$. Control systems analysis and design constantly refer to the mapping between the complex-variable plane, such as the s-plane, and the complex function plane, such as the $G(s)$ plane. Figure 6-2 illustrates

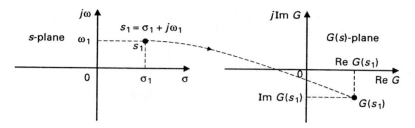

Figure 6-2. Mapping from the s-plane to the $G(s)$-plane.

the mapping of the point s_1 on to the point $G(s_1)$ in the complex function $G(s)$-plane. For example, the root-locus plot is a mapping of the real axis of the $G(s)$ onto the s-plane, because points on the root loci must satisfy $G(s) = -1/K$ for $-\infty < K < \infty$. The Nyquist plot for stability studies is a mapping of the $j\omega$-axis of the s-plane onto the $G(s)$-plane. The *CSAD Toolbox* contains functions that conduct various computations of complex-variable functions for the analysis and design of control systems.

6.2.3 Poles and Zeros of a Complex Function

Functions of the complex variable in linear control systems are usually found in the form of either a polynomial or a rational algebraic function in the form of a quotient of polynomials. These are illustrated as follows:

Polynomial:

$$P(s) = s^n + a_1 s^{n-1} + a_2 s^{n-1} + \ldots + a_{n-1}s + a_n \tag{6-3}$$

Rational Function:

$$G(s) = \frac{N(s)}{D(s)} \tag{6-4}$$

where $N(s)$ and $D(s)$ are polynomials of the form of Equation 6-3.

For systems with pure time delays, $G(s)$ may also contain a factor e^{-Ts}, where T is the time delay in seconds, and s is a complex variable.

A function $G(s)$ is said to be *analytical* in a given region of the s-plane if the function, and all its derivatives (with respect to s) exist in the region.

Zeros of a Complex Function: Given the function $G(s)$ that is analytic at $s = s_i$, it is said to have a zero of order r at $s = s_i$, if the limit

$$\lim_{s \to s_i} [(s - s_i)^{-r} G(s)] \tag{6-5}$$

has a finite, nonzero value. For example, the following function has a simple zero at $s = 1$ and a zero of order two at $s = -2$ and ∞.

$$G(s) = \frac{10(s - 1)(s + 2)^2}{s^2(s + 10)(s^2 + 2s + 2)} \tag{6-6}$$

Sec. 6.2   Complex Variables and Functions   **23**

Poles of a Complex Function: Given the function $G(s)$ that is analytic at $s = s_i$, it is said to have a pole of order r at $s = s_i$ if the limit

$$\lim_{s \to s_i} [(s - s_i)^r G(s)]$$

has a finite, nonzero value. For example, the function in Equation 6-6 has simple poles at $s = -10, -1 + j1$ and $-1 - j1$, and a pole of order two at $s = 0$.

6.3 DIFFERENTIAL EQUATIONS/STATE EQUATIONS

Because most physical systems contain energy-storage elements and components with memory, such as masses and springs in mechanical systems, capacitors and inductances in electrical systems, the mathematical models of these systems involve the use of differential equations. These equations generally involve derivatives and integrals of the dependent variables with respect to the independent variable. For instance, the differential equation that portrays the dynamics of a linear mechanical mass-spring-friction system is

$$M \frac{dy^2(t)}{dt^2} + B \frac{dy(t)}{dt} + Ky(t) = f(t) \tag{6-7}$$

where $f(t)$ is the applied force, M is the mass, B is the frictional coefficient, K is the linear spring constant, $y(t)$ is the displacement, and t is the independent variable, time.

The differential equation in Equation 6-7 is also known as a second-order ordinary differential equation, because the highest derivative involved is of the second order. In general, a linear nth-order differential equation is written

$$\frac{dy^n(t)}{dt^n} + a_n \frac{dy^{n-1}(t)}{dt^{n-1}} + \ldots + a_2 \frac{dy(t)}{dt} + a_1 y(t)$$

$$= b_{m+1} \frac{d^m r(t)}{dt^m} + b_m \frac{d^{m-1} r(t)}{dt^{m-1}} + \ldots + b_2 \frac{dr(t)}{dt} + b_1 r(t) \tag{6-8}$$

and the system it portrays is called a linear nth-order system. The coefficients $a_1, a_2, \ldots, a_n$ and $b_1, b_2, \ldots, b_{m+1}$ are real constants in this case.

6.3.1 State Equations

In general, an nth-order differential equation can be decomposed into n first-order differential equations. In principle, first-order differential equations are simpler to solve than high-order ones. They are also simpler to represent in the matrix form. This is why MATLAB uses the first-order differential equations format for data input.

Consider that a SISO linear time-invariant system is modeled by the following second-order differential equation:

$$\frac{d^2 y(t)}{dt^2} + a_2 \frac{dy(t)}{dt} + a_1 y(t) = u(t) \tag{6-9}$$

where a_1 and a_2 are real constants, $y(t)$ is the system output, and $u(t)$ is the input. Let us define

$$x_1(t) = y(t) \tag{6-10}$$

and

$$x_2(t) = \frac{dy(t)}{dt} = \frac{dx_1(t)}{dt} \tag{6-11}$$

Substituting the last two equations into Equation 6-9, we get two first-order differential equations.

$$\frac{dx_1(t)}{dt} = x_2(t) \tag{6-12}$$

$$\frac{dx_2(t)}{dt} = -a_1 x_1(t) - a_2 x_2(t) + u(t) \tag{6-13}$$

The variables $x_1(t)$ and $x_2(t)$ are defined as the *state variables*. The first-order differential equations are called *state equations*. In vector-matrix form, the two state equations in Equations 6-12 and 6-13 are expressed as

$$\frac{d\mathbf{x}(t)}{dt} = \mathbf{A}\mathbf{x}(t) + \mathbf{B}u(t) \tag{6-14}$$

where $\mathbf{x}(t)$ is defined as the *state vector* and is the column matrix

$$\mathbf{x}(t) = \begin{bmatrix} x_1(t) \\ x_2(t) \end{bmatrix} \tag{6-15}$$

A and **B** are called the *coefficient matrices*,

$$\mathbf{A} = \begin{bmatrix} 0 & 1 \\ -a_1 & -a_2 \end{bmatrix} \tag{6-16}$$

$$\mathbf{B} = \begin{bmatrix} 0 \\ 1 \end{bmatrix} \tag{6-17}$$

In this case the output $y(t)$ is linked to the state variables through Equation 6-10. We can define the *output equation* as

$$y(t) = x_1(t) \tag{6-18}$$

In general, the output may also depend on the input $u(t)$ directly, so that the vector-matrix output equation is written

$$\mathbf{y}(t) = \mathbf{Cx}(t) + \mathbf{Du}(t) \qquad (6\text{-}19)$$

where $\mathbf{y}(t)$ is the *output vector*; $\mathbf{C}$ and $\mathbf{D}$ are coefficient matrices with appropriate dimensions. For the output equation in Equation 6-18, $\mathbf{C}$ is

$$\mathbf{C} = [1 \quad 0] \qquad (6\text{-}20)$$

The state equation in Equation 6-14 and the output equation in Equation 6-19 are collectively called the *dynamic equations*.

A more formal discussion on state-variable representation of linear time-invariant systems is given in Chapter 7.

The programs `svplot` and `svstuff` of the *CSAD Toolbox* can be used to solve linear state equations for SISO systems with a unit-step input and zero initial conditions.

6.4 TRANSFER FUNCTIONS (SISO SYSTEMS)

Linear classical control systems theory is based on the use of transfer functions to describe the relationship between the input and the output. One way of defining the transfer function of a linear time-invariant system is to use the impulse response. The *impulse response* $g(t)$ of a linear SISO system is defined as the output $y(t)$ when the input $r(t)$ is a unit-impulse function $\delta(t)$, with all the initial conditions set to zero. The transfer function is defined as the Laplace transform of the impulse response; that is,

$$G(s) = \mathcal{L}[g(t)] \qquad (6\text{-}21)$$

where $\mathcal{L}$ denotes the Laplace operator.

Once the transfer function of a linear system is known, the input and output of the system is related through

$$G(s) = \frac{Y(s)}{R(s)} \qquad (6\text{-}22)$$

where $R(s)$ and $Y(s)$ are the Laplace transform of the input $r(t)$ and the output $y(t)$, respectively. The initial conditions of the system are set to zero.

Consider that an nth-order linear SISO system is described by the differential equation in Equation 6-8. To obtain the transfer function of the system, we take the Laplace transform on both sides of the system differential equation, set the initial conditions to zero, and take the ratio between the output and the input. The result is

$$G(s) = \frac{Y(s)}{R(s)} = \frac{b_{m+1}s^m + b_m s^{m-1} + \ldots + b_2 s + b_1}{s^n + a_n s^{n-1} + \ldots + a_2 s + a_1} \qquad (6\text{-}23)$$

A system with a transfer function that satisfies the $m \leq n$ condition is called a *proper system*. When $m = n$, the transfer function has a constant term, which means that the output will have the same property when the input has a jump discontinuity. Most physical systems are described by transfer functions with $n > m$. These systems are termed *strictly proper*.

6.4.1 Transfer Functions with Time Delays

Most MATLAB operations dealing with transfer functions handle only rational functions. For systems with pure time delays, the transfer function contains the delay function e^{-Ts}, where T is the time delay in seconds. The *CSAD Toolbox* function tfdelay gives Pade's approximation of the time-delay once the values of T and the order M of the approximating polynomial are given. For example, entering the following command at the MATLAB prompt

```
>>[N,D]=tfdelay(T,M,1) <CR>
```

where $<CR>$ denotes carriage return or the **enter** key on the keyboard, gives an Mth-order Pade's approximation of e^{-Ts} with the denominator order greater than the numerator order by one. The command [N,D]=tfdelay(T,M) gives a Pade's approximation with the numerator and denominator polynomials of the same order.

As an illustrative example,

```
>>[N,D]=tfdelay(0.1,2,1) <CR>
```

gives the following results for $T = 0.1$ and $M = 2$:

```
N =
      -20        600
D =
     1     40     600
```

The approximation function is

$$e^{-0.1s} \cong \frac{-20s + 600}{s^2 + 40s + 600} \tag{6-24}$$

```
>>[N,D]=tfdelay(0.1,2) <CR>


N =
     1    -60    1200
D =
     1     60    1200
```

which corresponds to

$$e^{-0.1s} \cong \frac{s^2 - 60s + 1200}{s^2 + 60s + 1200} \qquad (6\text{-}25)$$

The following results are obtained for $T = 0.1$ and $M = 3$:

```
>>[N,D]=tfdelay(0.1,3,1) <CR>


N =
    30   -2400   6000
D =
    1      90    3600   6000
```

which corresponds to

$$e^{-0.1s} \cong \frac{30s^2 - 2400s + 60000}{s^3 + 90s^2 + 3600s + 60000} \qquad (6\text{-}26)$$

For frequency-response plots of the transfer function $N(s)/D(s)$ that has a pure time delay factor, *CSAD Toolbox* functions handle e^{-Ts} in its exact form, because the term e^{-Ts} contributes a pure phase shift to the phase plot, and there is no effect on the magnitude plot.

6.4.2 The Characteristic Equation

The characteristic equation of a linear system is defined as the equation obtained by setting the denominator polynomial of the transfer function to zero. For the transfer function in Equation 6-23, the characteristic equation is

$$s^n + a_n s^{n-1} + \ldots + a_2 s + a_1 = 0 \qquad (6\text{-}27)$$

6.5 TIME RESPONSES WITH CSAD FUNCTIONS

Given the transfer function $G(s)$ of a linear system, the output response of the system that corresponds to an input $r(t)$, when the initial conditions are zero, is determined by taking the inverse Laplace transform of $G(s)R(s)$. The functions `iltplot` and `tftplot` can be used to compute the output response with transfer functions. Specifically, `tftplot` computes and plots the unit-step response of a linear system given the transfer function $G(s) = N(s)/D(s)$. The input data of $G(s)$ can be modified to provide impulse and ramp responses with the `tftplot`. The function `iltplot` computes and plots the inverse Laplace transform of any proper rational function. This means that `iltplot` can be used to compute the output response of a linear system with any input simply by entering the $N(s)/D(s)$ as the product of the transfer function and the input transform, $G(s)R(s)$. Illustrative examples on the applications of these programs are given subsequently.

6.5.1 Unit-Step Response with the `tftplot` Program

Consider that the output response of the system with the following transfer function is to be determined when the input is a unit-step function $u(t)$.

$$G(s) = \frac{Y(s)}{R(s)} = \frac{N(s)}{D(s)} = \frac{10}{s^2 + s + 10} \tag{6-28}$$

The function `tftplot` is executed by entering `tftplot`, followed by <CR>, at the MATLAB prompt >>. The program will respond by asking for the numerator and the denominator polynomials of the transfer function.

```
Default input is: 2
Enter Numerator polynomial > 10 <CR>
Default input is: s^2 + 2s^1 + 2
Enter Denominator polynomial > [1 1 10] <CR>
The options menu of tftplot will appear as follows:

            - TFTPLOT OPTIONS -

        Plot          Final time
        Zoom in        New TF
        Set axes       Display TF
        Grid plot      Attributes
        Hold plot      Roots
        Label Plot    View data
                       Quit

Option? >
```

Entering p <CR> at the `Option?` > prompt will bring the output response plot on the monitor screen, as shown in Fig. 6-3. The "Attributes" option gives the vital data on the unit-step response such as delay time, rise time, settling time, percent maximum overshoot, and peak time. These quantities will be described in detail in Section 8-4.

Explanations of all elements in the `tftplot` menu are found in Part 3: *CSAD Toolbox* Reference and are not elaborated on here. However, it is worthwhile to demonstrate the "Hold plot" option. Several plots can be superposed on the same set of axes simply by holding the plot and computing the responses consecutively. For instance, after plotting the unit-step response of Equation 6-28, enter h <CR> at the prompt >>. The program will respond:

```
Current plot held.
```

Then, enter n <CR> for "New T,F," and enter the transfer function,

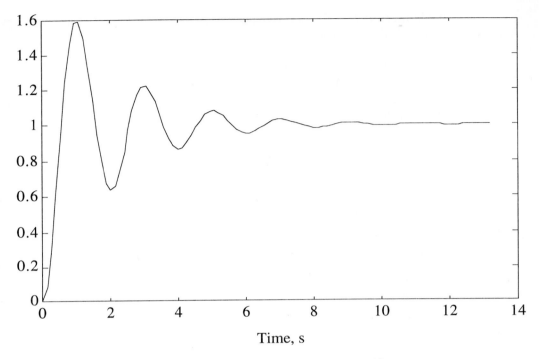

Figure 6-3. Unit-step response of $\dfrac{10}{s^2 + s + 10}$.

$$\frac{N(s)}{D(s)} = \frac{2}{s^2 + s + 2} \tag{6-29}$$

and execute plot; the step response of the system of Equation 6-29 will be displayed along with that of Equation 6-28, as shown in Figure 6-4.

Care should be taken in plotting multiple plots on the same set of axes. Once the "Final time" of the first plot is set, the "Final time" of subsequent plots must first be selected to be the same before plotting. Also, the bounds of the vertical axis of the plot must be set after the first plot to make certain that they will be sufficient to contain all subsequent plots.

The gain factor of $N(s)/D(s)$ can be adjusted accordingly for inputs with nonunity magnitudes.

6.5.2 Impulse Response with the `tftplot` Function

Because the impulse response of a linear system is simply the derivative of the unit-step response with respect to time, we can determine the former by entering the transfer function $sN(s)/D(s)$ to `tftplot`. For example, for the system transfer function given in Equation 6-28, we enter the polynomials $N(s)$ and $D(s)$ as follows:

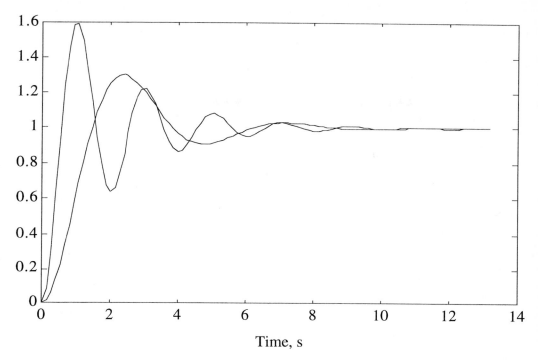

Figure 6-4. Unit-step responses of $\dfrac{10}{s^2 + s + 10}$ and $\dfrac{2}{s^2 + s + 2}$.

```
Enter numerator polynomial > [10 0] <CR>
Enter denominator polynomial > [1 1 10] <CR>
```

The impulse response of the system in Equation 6-28 is obtained as shown in Figure 6-5 using `tftplot` as the unit-step response of the following system:

$$\frac{N(s)}{D(s)} = \frac{10s}{s^2 + s + 10} \tag{6-30}$$

Warning: The "Attribute" option in `tftplot` does not work for the impulse response. It is intended only for unit-step responses.

6.5.3 Unit-ramp Response With the `tftplot` Function

The function `tftplot` can also be used for the computation of the unit-ramp response of a system given its transfer function. Because the Laplace transform of the unit-ramp function, $tu(t)$, is $1/s^2$, relative to the transform of the unit-step function $u(t)$, which is $1/s$, we can compute the unit-ramp response using `tftplot` simply by multiplying the transfer function by $1/s$. Thus, to obtain the unit-ramp response of Equation 6-28, we enter the transfer function

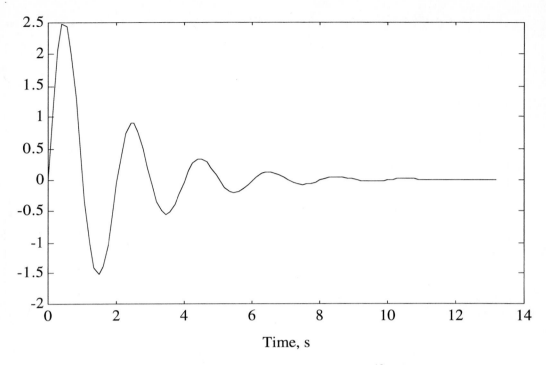

Figure 6-5. Impulse response of $\dfrac{10}{s^2 + s + 10}$.

$$\frac{N(s)}{D(s)} = \frac{10}{s(s^2 + s + 10)} \qquad (6\text{-}31)$$

The unit-ramp response is completed and plotted as shown in Figure 6-6.

6.5.4 The `iltplot` Function

The `iltplot` function computes and plots the inverse Laplace transform function of any proper function $N(s)/D(s)$. Thus, `iltplot` can be used to obtain the output response of linear systems with any input that has a rational Laplace transform. As an illustration, consider that the system with the transfer function in Equation 6-28 is subject to the input

$$r(t) = (1 + 2t)u(t) \qquad (6\text{-}32)$$

The Laplace transform of $r(t)$ is

$$R(s) = \frac{1}{s} + \frac{2}{s^2} = \frac{s(s + 2)}{s^2} \qquad (6\text{-}33)$$

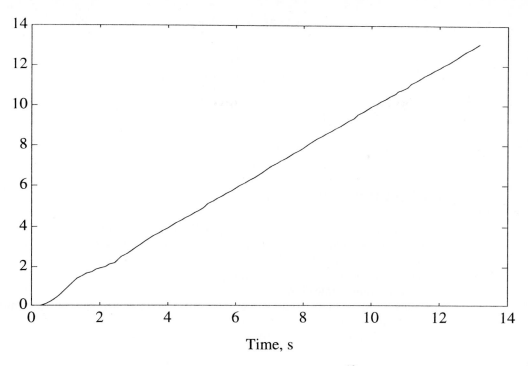

Figure 6-6. Unit-ramp response of $\dfrac{10}{s^2 + s + 10}$.

To apply `iltplot` to the computation of the output of the system in Equation 6-28, subject to the input described by Equation 6-33, we enter the transfer function

$$\frac{N(s)}{D(s)} = \frac{10s(s + 2)}{s^2(s^2 + s + 10)} = \frac{10(s + 2)}{s(s^2 + s + 10)} \qquad (6\text{-}34)$$

as input to `iltplot`. To execute `iltplot`, we enter `iltplot` <CR> at the MATLAB prompt >>. The function will prompt for the numerator polynomial $N(s)$ and the denominator polynomial $D(s)$:

```
Default input is: 2
Enter Numerator polynomial > 10*[1 2] <CR>
Default input is: s^2 + 2s^1 + 2
Enter Denominator polynomial > [1 1 10 0] <CR>
```

`iltplot` will display the following options menu:

Plot	Final time
Zoom in	New N, D
Set axes	Display
Grid plot	Roots
Hold plot	View data
Label plot	Quit

which is very similar to that of `tftplot`.

6.6 PARTIAL-FRACTION EXPANSION

Partial-fraction expansion is a tool that partitions a high-order transfer function into first- or second-order factors so that the inverse Laplace transform of the function can be evaluated from the Laplace transform table. The function `pfe` in CSAD computes the partial fraction expansion of $N(s)/D(s)$ and then displays the corresponding time-domain expression of each term. `pfe` cannot handle real poles of multiplicity greater than two and complex-conjugate poles of multiplicity greater than one.

For complex-conjugate poles, `pfe` returns a factor of the form of

$$\frac{K_1\beta^2}{(s + \alpha)^2 + \beta^2} \quad \text{and} \quad \frac{K_2(s + \alpha)}{(s + \alpha)^2 + \beta^2}$$

where K_1 and K_2 are constants rather than in two first-order terms. The reason is that the inverse Laplace transform of these second-order forms are readily available in standard Laplace transform table.

As an illustrative example, the partial-fraction expansion of the following function will be conducted using `pfe`.

$$\frac{N(s)}{D(s)} = \frac{20(s + 10)}{s(s + 2)^2(s^2 + 10s + 100)} \tag{6-35}$$

The function can be initiated by typing `pfe <CR>` at the MATLAB prompt or by first entering the numerator and denominator polynomials, $N(s)$ and $D(s)$, respectively. Entering `pfe <CR>` at the MATLAB prompt, the program responds:

```
Enter Numerator polynomial vector >20*[1 10] <CR>
Enter Denominator polynomial vector >pmult([1 0],[1 2],[1 2],
[1 10 100])<CR>
```

The output of `pfe` is

```
Terms in the partial fraction expansion are:
Complex Conjugate Pole at: -5.000 +/- j8.660
```

$$\frac{(0.02721)(s+5\ \ \ \ \ )}{(s+5\ \ \ \ \ )^2+(8.66\ \ \ \ )^2}$$

$$\frac{(0.003928)(8.66)}{(s+5\ \ \ \ \ )^2+(8.66\ \ \ \ )^2}$$

```
Time Domain: 0.02721*exp(-5t)*cos(8.66t)*u(t)
           + 0.003828*exp(-5t)*sin(8.66t)*u(t)
Double pole on Real Axis at: -2.000
```

$$\frac{-0.5272}{s+2}\ +\ \frac{-0.9524}{(s+2\ \ \ )^2}$$

```
Time Domain: -0.5272*exp(-2t)*u(t)
            -0.9524*exp(-2t)*u(t)
```

```
Pole at the origin:
```

$$\frac{0.5}{s}$$

```
Time Domain: 0.5*u(t)
Partial Fraction Expansion Complete
```

6.7 BLOCK DIAGRAMS AND SIGNAL FLOW GRAPHS

Block diagrams are often used in control systems analysis to relate the relationship between the transfer functions of interconnected systems and subsystems. Together with the transfer functions, block diagrams may be used to describe the algebraic relationship between the individual components of a system. Signal flow graphs on the other hand may be regarded simply as an alternative visual presentation to the block diagram. The algebraic laws of block diagrams and signal flow graphs are essentially the same.

Figure 6-7 illustrates the series and parallel connections of two SISO systems with transfer functions $G(s)$ and $H(s)$. For the series connection, the transfer function of the combined system is

$$\frac{Y(s)}{R(s)} = G(s)H(s) \tag{6-36}$$

For the parallel-connected systems, the transfer function of the overall system is

$$\frac{Y(s)}{R(s)} = G(s) + H(s) \tag{6-37}$$

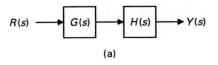

(a)

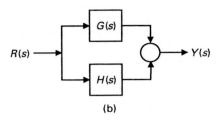

(b)

Figure 6-7. (a) Block diagram of two systems connected in cascade. (b) Block diagram of two systems connected in parallel.

Figure 6-8 shows the block diagram of two subsystems connected in a negative-feedback configuration. The transfer function of the overall system is

$$\frac{Y(s)}{R(s)} = \frac{G(s)}{1 + G(s)H(s)} \tag{6-38}$$

The equivalent signal flow graphs of the block diagrams in Figures 6-7 and 6-8 are shown in Figure 6-9.

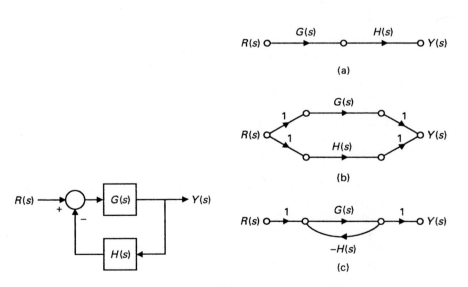

Figure 6-8. Block diagram of two systems connected in a negative-feedback configuration.

Figure 6-9. (a) Signal flow graph of two systems connected in cascade. (b) Signal flow graph of two systems connected in parallel. (c) Signal flow graph of two systems connected in a negative-feedback configuration.

Chap. 6   Mathematical Foundation

6.7.1 Manipulating Block Diagrams with `tfseries`, `tfparall`, and `tfcloop`

The *CSAD Toolbox* contains functions that perform the series, parallel, and feedback connections of two transfer functions $G(s)$ and $H(s)$. These programs are the `tfseries` (series), the `tfparall` (parallel), and `tfcloop` (feedback). The following transfer functions are used as an illustrative example.

$$G(s) = \frac{N_G(s)}{D_G(s)} = \frac{10}{s(s+1)(s+2)} \tag{6-39}$$

$$H(s) = \frac{N_H(s)}{D_H(s)} = \frac{s+4}{s+5} \tag{6-40}$$

To initiate any one of these programs, we must first enter the numerator and denominator polynomials of $G(s)$ and $H(s)$ at the MATLAB prompt

```
>> ng = 10; <CR>
>> dg = pmult([1 0], [1 1], [1 2]); <CR>
>> nh = [1 4]; <CR>
>> dh = [1 5]; <CR>
```

To get the series connection of $G(s)$ and $H(s)$, enter the following:

```
>>[N,D]=tfseries(ng,dg,nh,dh) <CR>
```

The program returns:

```
N =
    10   40
D =
    1    8    17   10   0
```

If the following command is entered at the >> prompt, the program returns the transfer function expression.

```
>>tfseries(ng,dg,ng,dh) <CR>
Composite Transfer function is:

            10s^1 + 40
    ----------------------------
    s^4 + 8s^3 + 17s^2 + 10s^1
```

To get the parallel connection of $G(s)$ and $H(s)$, enter the following:

```
>>[N,D]=tfparall(ng,dg,nh,dh) <CR>
```

The program returns

```
N =
    1   7   14   18   50
D =
    1   8   17   10   0
```

which corresponds to the transfer function,

$$\frac{s^4 + 7s^3 + 14s^2 + 18s^1 + 50}{s^4 + 8s^3 + 17s^2 + 10s^1}$$

To get the feedback connection of $G(s)$ and $H(s)$, enter the following:

```
>> tfcloop(ng,dg,nh,dh) <CR>
```

The program returns

```
Composite Transfer Function is:
```

$$\frac{10*(s^1 + 50)}{s^4 + 8s^3 + 17s^2 + 20s^1 + 40}$$

6.7.2 Feedback Systems with Constant Feedback

When the feedback system in Figure 6-8 has a constant feedback, that is, $H(s) = k$, where k is a real constant. The transfer function of the overall system can be obtained simply by entering `[N,D]=tfcloop(nl,dl,k) <CR>`, where `nl` and `dl` are the polynomial vectors of the numerator and denominator of $G(s)$, respectively.

6.7.3 Multiple-Loop Systems

For systems with multiple loops or more complex configurations than those shown in Figure 6-8, the functions `tfseries`, `tfparall`, and `tfcloop` can be applied repeatedly by identifying the overall system as an interconnection of subsystems. As an illustrative example, consider the block diagram shown in Figure 6-10. For reference purposes, the blocks of the system are identified as subsystems. The overall feedback gain is unity.

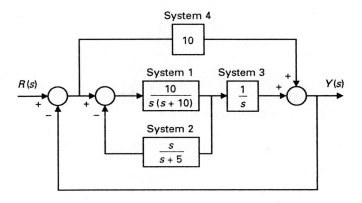

Figure 6-10. A multiple-loop feedback system.

The following data are first entered:

```
>> n1=10; <CR>
>> d1=[1 10 0]; <CR>
>> n2=[1 0]; <CR>
>> d2=[1 5]; <CR>
>> n3=1; <CR>
>> d3=[1 0]; <CR>
>> n4=10; <CR>
>> d4=1; <CR>
>> k=1
```

The commands are given so that the resulting numerator and denominator polynomials of each step are used for the next step without having to reenter the data.

```
>> [N,D]=tfcloop(n1,d1,n2,d2) <CR>
N =
    10  50
D =
    1  15  60  0
>> [N,D]=tfseries(N,D,n3,d3) <CR>
N =
    10  50
D =
    1  15  60  0  0
>> [N,D]=tfparall(N,D,n4,d4) <CR>

 N =
    10  150  600  10  50
```

```
D =
      1    15    60    0    0
>> tfcloop(N,D,k) <CR>
Composite Transfer Function is
            10*(s^4 + 15s^3 + 60s^2 + s^1 + 5)
-------------------------------------------------------
11*(s^4 + 15s^3 + 60s^2 + 0.9091s^1 + 4.545)
```

6.7.4 The State Diagram

When a linear system is described by dynamic equations, the block diagram of signal flow graph representation of the dynamic equations is called a *state diagram*. For example, the state diagram of the dynamic equations in Equations 6-12, 6-13, and 6-18 is drawn as shown in Figure 6-11. The branches with gain s^{-1} denoted integration with respect to time because $s^{-1}X(s)$ is the Laplace transform representation of the integral of $x(t)$ with respect to t. The function svstuff contains many options that can be used for the analysis and design of linear SISO systems portrayed in the state-variable form. Details of the state-variable analysis are given in Chapter 7.

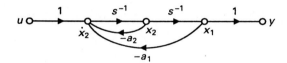

Figure 6-11. State diagram of the system modeled by Equations 6-12, 6-13, and 6-18.

EXERCISES

6-1. Given the following two polynomials:

$$a = s^2 + 3.2s + 5$$

$$b = s - 12$$

(a) Use the function pmult to obtain the product of the two polynomials.
   Answer: [1.0000 −8.8000 −33.4000 −60.0000]
(b) Use the function padd to obtain the sum of the two polynomials.
   Answer: [1.0000 4.2000 −7.0000]

6-2. Use the function pzshow to find the poles and zeros of the following transfer functions:

(a)
$$\frac{N(s)}{D(s)} = \frac{10(s^2 + 10s + 1)}{s^2(s^2 + 5s + 5)}$$

Answer: zeros: −9.8990 −0.1010 ∞ ∞
        poles: 0   0 −3.6180 −1.3820

(b)
$$\frac{N(s)}{D(s)} = \frac{10(s^2 + 3s + 2)}{(s + 10)(s^3 + 2s + 1)}$$

Answer: zeros: $-2.0000 \quad -1.0000 \quad \infty \quad \infty$
poles: $\quad 0.2267 + 1.4677i$
$\qquad 0.2267 - 1.4677i$
$\qquad -0.4534 - 10.000$

6-3. For the following input-output transfer function:

(a) Find the unit-step response using `tftplot`. Find all the attributes of the step response and the roots of the characteristic equation.

(b) Find the impulse response of the system with `tftplot`.

(c) Find the response of the system with `tftplot` when the input is a unit-ramp function, $tu(t)$.

(i)

$$\frac{N(s)}{D(s)} = \frac{10(s + 5)}{(s + 1)(s^2 + 5s + 50)}$$

(ii)

$$\frac{N(s)}{D(s)} = \frac{10(s^2 + s + 10)}{(s + 10)^2(s^2 + s + 1)}$$

6-4. Using `iltplot`, find the output responses of the systems described in Problem 6-3, with the following inputs:

(a)
$$r(t) = (1 + 0.2t)u(t)$$

(b)
$$r(t) = (1 + 0.2t + 0.2t^2)u(t)$$

6-5. Find the unit-step response of the system with the following transfer function by using `tftplot`:

$$\frac{N(s)}{D(s)} = \frac{e^{-Ts}}{s^2 + s + 1}$$

Use the `tfdelay` program to obtain an Mth-order approximation of e^{-Ts} with $T = 1$ s. Use $M = 1$ and then $M = 2$. Plot the step responses of the system with $T = 0$ s, and then with $T = 1$ s, $M = 1$, and $M = 2$. Comment on the accuracy of the approximation of the time delay when M is increased from 1 to 2. Repeat the problem using `tfdelay(T,M,1)`.

6-6. Given the following transfer functions:

$$G(s) = \frac{N_G(s)}{D_G(s)} = \frac{100(s + 1)}{s(s + 1.5)(s + 20)}$$

$$H(s) = \frac{N_H(s)}{D_H(s)} = \frac{s}{s + 1}$$

(a) Find the overall transfer function of the system with $G(s)$ and $H(s)$ connected in series. Use `tfseries`.

(b) Find the overall transfer function of the system with $G(s)$ and $H(s)$ connected in parallel. Use `tfparall`.

(c) Find the overall transfer function of the closed-loop systems with negative feedback, with $G(s)$ in the forward path and $H(s)$ in the feedback path. Use `tfcloop`.

6-7. The block diagram of a feedback control system is shown in Figure 6P-7. Find the transfer function $Y(s)/R(s)$ by applying the functions `tfseries` and `tfcloop` repeatedly.

Answer: $N = 1 \quad 1 \qquad D = 1 \quad 2 \quad 3 \quad 4 \quad 1$

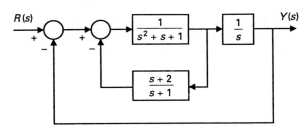

Figure 6P-7.

6-8. The block diagram of a feedback control system is shown in Figure 6P-8. Find the transfer function $Y(s)/R(s)$ by applying the functions `tfseries`, `tfparall`, and `tfcloop` repeatedly.

Answer: $N = 5 \quad 10 \quad 15 \quad 16 \quad 1 \qquad D = 6 \quad 12 \quad 18 \quad 19 \quad 1$

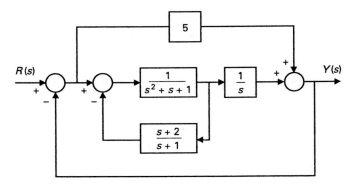

Figure 6P-8.

7

State-Variable Analysis

7.1 INTRODUCTION

State-variable representation of control systems is more modern than the transfer function approach because linear and nonlinear systems, time-invariant and time-varying systems, and single-variable and multivariable systems can all be modeled in a unified manner. Optimal control theory often depends on the system being modeled by state-variable formulation. A system that is modeled by its state-variable model is more readily analyzed by computer means. In fact, time responses computed by *CSAD Toolbox* functions are always carried out by converting transfer functions to state variable representations. The reader should be familiar with the basic concepts and applications of the state-variable analysis. Important subjects include various state transformations, the relationship between the transfer function and state-variable formulations, controllability, and observability.

7.2 THE STATE-VARIABLE FORMULATION

The state equations of an nth-order linear time-invariant system can be expressed as

$$\frac{d\mathbf{x}(t)}{dt} = \mathbf{Ax}(t) + \mathbf{Bu}(t) \qquad (7\text{-}1)$$

where $\mathbf{x}(t)$ is the *state vector*, which is an $n \times 1$ vector.

$$\mathbf{x}(t) = \begin{bmatrix} x_1(t) \\ x_2(t) \\ \vdots \\ x_n(t) \end{bmatrix} \qquad (7\text{-}2)$$

The $n \times n$ coefficient matrix $\mathbf{A}$ is written

$$\mathbf{A} = \begin{bmatrix} a_{11} & a_{12} & \cdots & a_{1n} \\ a_{21} & a_{22} & \cdots & a_{2n} \\ \vdots & \vdots & \vdots\vdots & \vdots \\ a_{n1} & a_{n2} & \cdots & a_{nn} \end{bmatrix} \qquad (7\text{-}3)$$

where the elements are real constants. The matrix $\mathbf{B}$ is $n \times p$ with constant elements:

$$\mathbf{B} = \begin{bmatrix} b_{11} & b_{12} & \cdots & b_{1p} \\ b_{21} & b_{22} & \cdots & b_{2p} \\ \vdots & \vdots & \vdots\vdots & \vdots \\ b_{n1} & b_{n2} & \cdots & b_{np} \end{bmatrix} \qquad (7\text{-}4)$$

The *input vector* $\mathbf{u}(t)$ is denoted by the $p \times 1$ vector

$$\mathbf{u}(t) = \begin{bmatrix} u_1(t) \\ u_2(t) \\ \vdots \\ u_p(t) \end{bmatrix} \qquad (7\text{-}5)$$

The *output equations* represent the relationship between the outputs and the state variables and inputs, and are written in matrix form as

$$\mathbf{y}(t) = \mathbf{Cx}(t) + \mathbf{Du}(t) \qquad (7\text{-}6)$$

where $\mathbf{y}(t)$ is the $q \times 1$ *output vector*,

$$\mathbf{y(t)} = \begin{bmatrix} y_1(t) \\ y_2(t) \\ \vdots \\ y_q(t) \end{bmatrix} \qquad (7\text{-}7)$$

The coefficient matrix $\mathbf{C}$ that relates the outputs and the state variables is $q \times n$, and is written as

$$\mathbf{C} = \begin{bmatrix} c_{11} & c_{12} & \cdots & c_{1n} \\ c_{21} & c_{22} & \cdots & c_{2n} \\ \vdots & \vdots & \vdots\vdots\vdots & \vdots \\ c_{q1} & c_{q2} & \cdots & c_{qn} \end{bmatrix} \qquad (7\text{-}8)$$

The coefficient matrix $\mathbf{D}$ contains elements that relate the inputs directly to the outputs, and is $q \times p$; $\mathbf{D}$ is written as

$$\mathbf{D} = \begin{bmatrix} d_{11} & d_{12} & \cdots & d_{1p} \\ d_{21} & d_{22} & \cdots & d_{2p} \\ \vdots & \vdots & \vdots\vdots\vdots & \vdots \\ d_{q1} & d_{q2} & \cdots & d_{qp} \end{bmatrix} \qquad (7\text{-}9)$$

The state equations in Equation 7-1 and the output equations of Equation 7-6 are collectively called the *dynamic equations*.

7.3 THE SVSTUFF FUNCTION

The function svstuff in the *CSAD Toolbox* is a menu-driven program that can be used to perform various computations related to the state-variable analysis and design of SISO linear time-invariant systems.

Details and descriptions of svstuff are given in Part 3: *CSAD Toolbox* Reference. Typing svstuff, followed by <CR> at the MATLAB prompt >>, the svstuff menu appears as follows:

```
                    -SVSTUFF-
        Eigenvalues         Response to step
        Controllability     Display A,B,C,D
        Observability       New A,B,C,D
        Transformations     Find N(s)/D(s)
        State feedback      Input N(s)/D(s)
                            Quit
```

Choose Option *N* (New **A, B, C, D**) or *I* (Input $N(s)/D(s)$) to `Enter a system`.

After the system is entered in either state-variable or transfer function form the menu reappears.

7.4 CHARACTERISTIC EQUATION AND EIGENVALUES

The characteristic equation of **A** is defined as

$$\det(s\mathbf{I} - \mathbf{A}) = \left| s\mathbf{I} - \mathbf{A} \right| = 0 \qquad (7\text{-}10)$$

The *eigenvalues* of **A** are the roots of the characteristic equation. It should be noted that the characteristic polynomial $\left| s\mathbf{I} - \mathbf{A} \right|$ is also the denominator polynomial $D(s)$ of the input-output transfer function $N(s)/D(s)$ if the `Find N(s)/D(s)` option is selected from the `svstuff` menu. Consider that a second-order system is described by the following coefficient matrices:

$$\mathbf{A} = \begin{bmatrix} 0 & 1 \\ -10 & -1 \end{bmatrix} \qquad \mathbf{B} = \begin{bmatrix} 0 \\ 1 \end{bmatrix} \qquad \mathbf{C} = [1 \quad 0] \qquad \mathbf{D} = 0 \qquad (7\text{-}11)$$

Selecting the `Find N(s)/D(s)` option, the returned input-output transfer function is

$$\frac{1}{s^2 + s + 10} \qquad (7\text{-}12)$$

Thus, the characteristic equation is

$$s^2 + s + 10 = 0 \qquad (7\text{-}13)$$

Selecting the `Eigenvalues` option from the `svstuff` menu, the function returns

```
Eigenvalues of A are:
        −0.5000 + 3.1225i
        −0.5000 − 3.1225i
```

7.5 STATE TRANSFORMATIONS

Several similarity transformations are useful in the state-variable analysis and design of linear systems. These are the *controllable canonical form* (CCF), the *observable canonical form* (OCF), and the *diagonal form* (DF).

The *Jordan canonical form* for multiple-order eigenvalues is not treated here.

7.5.1 Controllable Canonical Form (CCF)

Consider that the state equations in Equation 7-1 describe a linear system with a single input; this is, $u(t)$ is a scalar, and $\mathbf{B}$ is a column matrix.

If the matrices $\mathbf{A}$ and $\mathbf{B}$ satisfy the following rank condition,

$$R[\mathbf{B} \ \mathbf{AB} \ \mathbf{A}^2\mathbf{B} \ \mathbf{A}^3\mathbf{B} \ \cdots \ \mathbf{A}^{n-1}\mathbf{B}] = n \tag{7-14}$$

where R represents "the rank of," then there exists a transformation

$$\mathbf{x} = \mathbf{T}\bar{\mathbf{x}} \tag{7-15}$$

that transforms the state equations to

$$\frac{d\bar{\mathbf{x}}(t)}{dt} = \overline{\mathbf{A}}\mathbf{x}(t) + \overline{\mathbf{B}}u(t) \tag{7-16}$$

where the coefficient matrices in the CCF form are given as

$$\overline{\mathbf{A}} = \begin{bmatrix} 0 & 1 & 0 & 0 & \cdots & 0 \\ 0 & 0 & 1 & 0 & \cdots & 0 \\ 0 & 0 & 0 & 1 & \cdots & 0 \\ \cdot & \cdot & \cdot & \cdot & \cdots & \cdot \\ 0 & 0 & 0 & 0 & \cdots & 1 \\ -a_1 & -a_2 & -a_3 & -a_4 & \cdots & -a_{n'} \end{bmatrix} = \mathbf{T}^{-1}\mathbf{A}\mathbf{T} \tag{7-17}$$

$$\overline{\mathbf{B}} = \begin{bmatrix} 0 \\ 0 \\ 0 \\ \vdots \\ 0 \\ 1 \end{bmatrix} = \mathbf{T}^{-1}\mathbf{B} \tag{7-18}$$

The output equation in Equation 7-2 is transformed to

$$\bar{\mathbf{y}}(t) = \overline{\mathbf{C}}\mathbf{x}(t) + \mathbf{D}u(t) \tag{7-19}$$

where

$$\overline{\mathbf{C}} = \mathbf{C}\mathbf{T} \tag{7-20}$$

CCF is also known as *phase-variable canonical form* (PVCF). As will be discussed later, a system in CCF is always controllable.

7.5.2 Observable Canonical Form (OCF)

Observable canonical form (OCF) refers to the transformation in Equation 7-15 that transforms Equations 7-1 and 7-2 to Equations 7-16 and 7-19, respectively, with

$$\overline{\mathbf{A}} = \begin{bmatrix} 0 & 0 & 0 & \cdots & 0 & -a_1 \\ 1 & 0 & 0 & \cdots & 0 & -a_2 \\ 0 & 1 & 0 & \cdots & 0 & -a_3 \\ \cdot & \cdot & \cdot & \cdots & \cdot & \cdot \\ 0 & 0 & 0 & \cdots & 0 & -a_{n-1} \\ 0 & 0 & 0 & \cdots & 1 & -a_n \end{bmatrix} \qquad (7\text{-}21)$$

$$\overline{\mathbf{B}} = \mathbf{T}^{-1}\mathbf{B} \qquad (7\text{-}22)$$

$$\overline{\mathbf{C}} = [0 \quad 0 \quad 0 \quad \cdots \quad 0 \quad 1] \qquad (7\text{-}23)$$

The condition that the OCF transformation can be carried out is that the matrices **A** and **C** must satisfy the following rank condition:

$$R \begin{bmatrix} \mathbf{C} \\ \mathbf{CA} \\ \mathbf{CA}^2 \\ \vdots \\ \mathbf{CA}^{n-1} \end{bmatrix} = n \qquad (7\text{-}24)$$

Notice that the matrix $\overline{\mathbf{A}}$ of the OCF is the transpose of the $\overline{\mathbf{A}}$ in CCF in Equation 7-17, whereas $\overline{\mathbf{C}}$ for the OCF in Equation 7-23 is the transpose of $\overline{\mathbf{B}}$ of the CCF. OCF is also known as *dual phase-variable canonical form* (DPVCF). As will be discussed later, a system represented in OCF is always observable.

7.5.3 Diagonal Transformation

If the matrix **A** has distinct eigenvalues, a nonsingular transformation of the form of Equation 7-15 can be used to transform **A** into a diagonal matrix. That is, for the transformed state equation of Equation 7-16,

$$\overline{\mathbf{A}} = \mathbf{T}^{-1}\mathbf{A}\mathbf{T} = \begin{bmatrix} \lambda_1 & 0 & 0 & \cdots & 0 \\ 0 & \lambda_2 & 0 & \cdots & 0 \\ \cdot & \cdot & \cdot & \cdots & \cdot \\ 0 & 0 & 0 & \cdots & \lambda_n \end{bmatrix} \qquad (7\text{-}25)$$

where $\lambda_1, \lambda_2, \cdots, \lambda_n$ are the eigenvalues of $\mathbf{A}$, and

$$\overline{\mathbf{B}} = \mathbf{T}^{-1}\mathbf{B} \tag{7-26}$$

DF is also known as *modal form* (MF).

7.5.4 CCF, OCF, and DF Transformation Using `svstuff`

The function `svstuff` in the *CSAD Toolbox* can be used to find the transformations into CCF, OCF, and DF starting from the state-variable representation or transfer function representation.

Given the matrices $\mathbf{A}$, $\mathbf{B}$, $\mathbf{C}$, and $\mathbf{D}$ of the state-variable representation, selecting the "Transformations" option one can get the CCF, OCF, or DF state representation of the system. Keep in mind that the matrices $\mathbf{A}$, $\mathbf{B}$, $\mathbf{C}$, and $\mathbf{D}$ must satisfy the following conditions:

> For the CCF transformation, $\mathbf{A}$ and $\mathbf{B}$ must satisfy the rank condition of Equation 7-14.
> For the OCF transformation, $\mathbf{A}$ and $\mathbf{C}$ must satisfy the rank conditon of Equation 7-24.
> For the DF transformation, $\mathbf{A}$ must have distinct eigenvalues.

The following illustrative examples are given to demonstrate the applications of `svstuff` to state transformations.

The system matrices are given as

$$\mathbf{A} = \begin{bmatrix} -3 & 2 & 0 \\ -1 & 0 & 1 \\ -2 & -3 & -4 \end{bmatrix} \qquad \mathbf{B} = \begin{bmatrix} 0 \\ 0 \\ 1 \end{bmatrix} \qquad \mathbf{C} = [1 \quad 0 \quad 0] \qquad \mathbf{D} = 0 \tag{7-27}$$

Selecting the `Eigenvalues` option from the menu, the following eigenvalues of $\mathbf{A}$ are given:

```
-1.4476 + 1.7379i
-1.4476 - 1.7379i
-4.1049
```

Selecting the `Transformations` option from the menu, the program will prompt for the type of transformation:

```
Choose state transformation CCF OCF DF [c] >
```

The CCF transformation is found by entering <CR> at the cursor. The results are:

Transformation Matrix T is:

```
2  0  0
3  1  1
2  3  1
```

$$\bar{A} = T^{-1}AT \qquad \bar{B} = T^{-1}B \qquad \bar{C} = CT \qquad \bar{D} = D$$

Abar:

```
   0    1    0
   0    0    1
 -21  -17   -7
```

Bbar:

```
0
0
1
```

Cbar:

```
2  0  0
```

Dbar:

```
0
```
                                                                          (7-28)

In performing the CCF transformation, the program automatically checks the rank condition of Equation 7-14 and prints out an error message if the rank condition is not satisfied.

Selecting the OCF option, the results are the following:

Transformation Matrix T is:

```
  0    0    1
  0   0.5  -2
 0.5  -2   6.5
```

$$\bar{A} = T^{-1}AT \qquad \bar{B} = T^{-1}B \qquad \bar{C} = CT \qquad \bar{D} = D$$

Abar:

```
0  0  -21
1  0  -17
0  1   -7
```

Bbar:

$$2$$
$$0$$
$$0$$

Cbar:

$$0 \quad 0 \quad 1$$

Dbar:

$$0$$

(7-29)

For the DF transformation, the results are

Transformation matrix T is:

$$
\begin{matrix}
0.1575 + 0.4160i & 0.1575 - 0.4169i & 0.2889 \\
-0.2400 + 0.4604i & -0.2400 - 0.4604i & -0.1596 \\
-0.2953 - 0.6668i & -0.2953 + 0.6668i & 0.9440
\end{matrix}
$$

$$\overline{A} = T^{-1}AT \quad \overline{B} = T^{-1}B \quad \overline{C} = CT \quad \overline{D} = D$$

Abar:

$$
\begin{matrix}
-1.4476 + 1.7379i & 0.0000 - 0.0000i & 0.0000 + 0.0000i \\
0.0000 + 0.0000i & -1.4476 - 1.7379i & 0.0000 - 0.0000i \\
0.0000 + 0.0000i & 0.0000 + 0.0000i & -4.1049 + 0.0000i
\end{matrix}
$$

Bbar:

$$
\begin{matrix}
-0.3970 + 0.0879i \\
-0.3870 - 0.0879i \\
0.6867 - 0.0000i
\end{matrix}
$$

Cbar:

$$0.1575 + 0.4169i \quad 0.1575 - 0.4169i \quad 0.2889$$

Dbar:

$$0$$

(7-30)

In performing the DF transformation, the program automatically checks if the matrix **A** has distinct eigenvalues; if not, an error message will be given.

Sec. 7.5   State Transformations

7.6 RELATIONSHIPS BETWEEN STATE VARIABLES AND TRANSFER FUNCTIONS—DECOMPOSITION

The transfer function representation of linear time-invariant systems is closely related to the state-variable representation.

Consider the system that is represented by the dynamic equations of Equations 7-1 and 7-6. Taking the Laplace transform on both sides of the dynamic equations, setting the initial states to zero, and after simple matrix manipulations, the input-output transfer relationship in the Laplace domain is written

$$\mathbf{Y}(s) = [\mathbf{C}(s\mathbf{I} - \mathbf{A})^{-1}\mathbf{B} + \mathbf{D}]\mathbf{U}(s) \qquad (7\text{-}31)$$

where $\mathbf{Y}(s)$ and $\mathbf{U}(s)$ are the Laplace transforms of $\mathbf{y}(t)$ and $\mathbf{u}(t)$, respectively. Thus, given the matrices $\mathbf{A}$, $\mathbf{B}$, $\mathbf{C}$, $\mathbf{D}$ of the dynamic equations, the transfer function relationship of the system is given by Equation 7-32. Equations 7-11 and 7-12 already give an illustration of the process and how it can be computed with the svstuff function for SISO systems.

For SISO systems, the input-output transfer function can be written as

$$\frac{Y(s)}{U(s)} = \frac{c_{n+1}s^n + c_n s^{n-1} + \cdots + c_2 s + c_1}{s^n + a_n s^{n-1} + a_{n-1}s^{n-2} + \cdots + a_2 s + a_1} \qquad (7\text{-}32)$$

where we have assumed that the system is *proper*; that is, the order of the numerator does not exceed that of the denominator.

The process of going from the transfer function to the state equations is called *decomposition*. Given the transfer function, the corresponding state and output equations are not unique, because the results depend on how the state variables are defined. However, because the state variables represent a minimum set that describes the dynamics of a system, given the state and output equations, the corresponding transfer function is always unique.

In general, there are three decomposition schemes. These are, *direct decomposition*, *parallel decomposition*, and *cascade decomposition*. These are briefly described as follows.

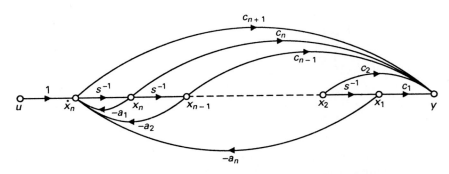

Figure 7-1. A state diagram of Equation 7-32 by direct decomposition.

7.6.1 Direct Decomposition

We can show that direct decomposition of a transfer function results in state-variable representation in the CCF. The state diagram of the system represented by Equation 7-32 is shown in Figure 7-1. The coefficient matrices of the dynamic equations are written,

$$
\mathbf{A} = \begin{bmatrix}
0 & 1 & 0 & 0 & \cdots & 0 \\
0 & 0 & 1 & 0 & \cdots & 0 \\
0 & 0 & 0 & 1 & \cdots & 0 \\
\cdot & \cdot & \cdot & \cdot & \cdots & \cdot \\
0 & 0 & 0 & 0 & \cdots & 1 \\
-a_1 & -a_2 & -a_3 & -a_4 & \cdots & -a_n
\end{bmatrix}
\tag{7-33}
$$

$$
\mathbf{B} = \begin{bmatrix}
0 \\
0 \\
0 \\
\vdots \\
0 \\
1
\end{bmatrix}
\tag{7-34}
$$

$$
\mathbf{C} = \begin{bmatrix} c_1 & c_2 & c_3 & \cdots & c_{n-1} & c_n \end{bmatrix}
\tag{7-35}
$$

$$
\mathbf{D} = c_{n+1}
\tag{7-36}
$$

Notice that if the system is *strictly proper*, that is, the order of the denominator polynomial is less than that of the numerator polynomial, then $\mathbf{D} = c_{n+1} = 0$.

Thus, direct decomposition of the transfer function in Equation 7-32 results in CCF in the state-variable representation.

For the OCF the Equation 7-21 shows that matrix $\mathbf{A}$ is simply the transpose of the $\mathbf{A}$ in Equation 7-33, $\mathbf{B}$ is equal to the transpose of the $\mathbf{C}$ in Equation 7-35, and Equation 7-23 shows that $\mathbf{C}$ is the transpose of the $\mathbf{B}$ in Equation 7-34. The matrix $\mathbf{D}$ is identical to that in Equation 7-36. The fact that given the transfer function $G(s)$ it can be decomposed into either CCF or OCF can be shown by writing the transfer function from Equation 7-31 as

$$G(s) = \mathbf{C}(s\mathbf{I} - \mathbf{A})^{-1}\mathbf{B} + \mathbf{D} \tag{7-37}$$

where $\mathbf{A}$, $\mathbf{B}$, $\mathbf{C}$, and $\mathbf{D}$ are in CCF. Because $G(s)$ is a scalar, taking the matrix transpose on both sides of Equation 7-37, we have

$$G(s) = [\mathbf{C}(s\mathbf{I} - \mathbf{A})^{-1}\mathbf{B} + \mathbf{D}]' \tag{7-38}$$
$$= [\mathbf{C}(s\mathbf{I} - \mathbf{A})^{-1}\mathbf{B}]' + \mathbf{D}'$$

Or

$$G(s) = \mathbf{B}'(s\mathbf{I} - \mathbf{A}')^{-1}\mathbf{C}' + \mathbf{D}' \tag{7-39}$$

Comparing Equation 7-37 with Equation 7-39, we see that the transfer function $G(s)$ is unchanged if $\mathbf{A}$, $\mathbf{B}$, $\mathbf{C}$, and $\mathbf{D}$ in Equation 7-37 are replaced by $\mathbf{A}'$, $\mathbf{C}'$, $\mathbf{B}'$, and $\mathbf{D}'$, respectively. The coefficient matrices in Equation 7-39 are in OCF.

7.6.2 Parallel Decomposition

By performing a parallel decomposition a transfer function can be represented in the DF if the system has distinct eigenvalues, and in the *Jordan canonical form* (JCF) if the system has at least one multiple-order eigenvalue. Analytically, the denominator polynomial of the transfer function should be in factored single-order form. The transfer function is then written as a sum of first-order factors by means of partial-fraction expansion. Consider that the transfer function of a linear SISO system with distinct eigenvalues is written as

$$\frac{Y(s)}{U(s)} = \frac{N(s)}{(s + \lambda_1)(s + \lambda_2) \cdots (s + \lambda_n)} \tag{7-40}$$

where the order of $N(s)$ is less than n. The eigenvalues $-\lambda_1, -\lambda_2, \cdots -\lambda_n$ can be real or in complex conjugate pairs. By partial-fraction expansion, $Y(s)/U(s)$ is written

$$\frac{Y(s)}{U(s)} = \frac{K_1}{s + \lambda_1} + \frac{K_2}{s + \lambda_2} + \cdots + \frac{K_n}{s + \lambda_n} \tag{7-41}$$

where K_1, K_2, $\cdots$ and K_n are real or complex coefficients.

The state diagram representation of Equation 7-41 is shown in Figure 7-2, where $b_i c_i = K_i$ for $i = 1, 2, \ldots, n$. Apparently, given the values of K_i, the values of b_i and c_i are not unique.

The coefficient matrices of the system in DF are written

$$\mathbf{A} = \begin{bmatrix} \lambda_1 & 0 & 0 & \cdots & 0 \\ 0 & \lambda_2 & 0 & \cdots & 0 \\ . & . & . & \cdots & . \\ 0 & 0 & 0 & \cdots & \lambda_n \end{bmatrix} \tag{7-42}$$

Chap. 7 State-Variable Analysis

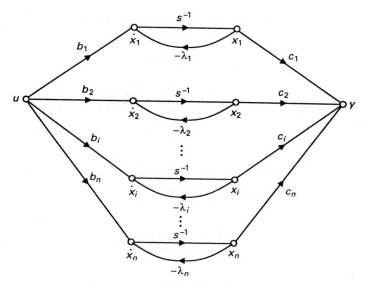

Figure 7-2. A state diagram of Equation 7-41 by parallel decomposition.

$$\mathbf{B} = \begin{bmatrix} b_1 \\ b_2 \\ \vdots \\ b_n \end{bmatrix} \qquad \mathbf{C} = [c_1 \quad c_2 \quad \cdots \quad c_n] \qquad \mathbf{D} = 0 \qquad (7\text{-}43)$$

When **A** has multiple-order eigenvalues, the state transformation is called JCF. Because the program DF does not handle the state-variable representation of systems with multiple-order eigenvalues, decomposition with JCF is not discussed here.

7.6.3 Cascade Decomposition

Cascade decomposition may be applied to a transfer function that is expressed as a series of subsystems. This means that the numerator and denominator polynomials must all be expressed in factored form.

Consider that the transfer function of a linear SISO system is expressed as

$$\frac{Y(s)}{U(s)} = \frac{K(s + \beta)}{(s + \lambda_1)(s + \lambda_2)} \qquad (7\text{-}44)$$

where K is a real constant, and there are no pole-zero cancellations. In this case the transfer function can be factored into two subsystems connected in cascade in several ways, two of which are shown below:

$$\frac{Y(s)}{U(s)} = \left(\frac{K}{(s + \lambda_1)}\right)\left(\frac{(s + \beta)}{(s + \lambda_2)}\right) \qquad (7\text{-}45)$$

or

$$\frac{Y(s)}{U(s)} = \left(\frac{(s + \beta)}{(s + \lambda_1)}\right)\left(\frac{K}{(s + \lambda_2)}\right) \qquad (7\text{-}46)$$

Figure 7-3 shows the state diagrams of the two systems portrayed by Equations 7-45 and 7-46. The coefficient matrices of the two systems in Figure 7-3 are given subsequently.

For Equation 7-45 and Figure 7-3(a)

$$\mathbf{A} = \begin{bmatrix} -\lambda_2 & 1 \\ 0 & -\lambda_1 \end{bmatrix} \qquad \mathbf{B} = \begin{bmatrix} 0 \\ K \end{bmatrix} \qquad \mathbf{C} = [\beta - \lambda_2 \ \ 1] \qquad \mathbf{D} = 0 \quad (7\text{-}47)$$

For Equation 7-46 and Figure 7-3(b)

$$\mathbf{A} = \begin{bmatrix} -\lambda_1 & \beta K \\ 0 & -\lambda_2 \end{bmatrix} \qquad \mathbf{B} = \begin{bmatrix} K \\ 1 \end{bmatrix} \qquad \mathbf{C} = [1 \ \ 0] \qquad \mathbf{D} = 0 \quad (7\text{-}48)$$

Because a transfer function can usually be factored and partitioned in a number of ways, the result of cascade decomposition is almost never unique.

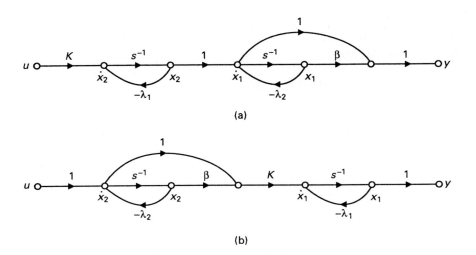

(a)

(b)

Figure 7-3. (a) State diagram of Equation 7-45. (b) State diagram of Equation 7-46.

7.6.4 Decomposition with `svstuff`

The "Input $N(s)/D(s)$" option of `svstuff` allows the user to input a transfer function $N(s)/D(s)$, and the state-variable representation in either CCF or OCF may be obtained. Then, by choosing the `Transformations` option, the DF can also be obtained.

Entering i followed by <CR> and the `Option?` > prompt, the transfer function

$$\frac{2}{s^3 + 7s^2 + 17s + 21}$$

is entered as follows:

```
Enter Numerator Polynomial > 2 <CR>
Enter Denominator Polynomial > [1 7 17 21] <CR>
Controllable or Observable Form? [c] >
```

By entering <CR> or o <CR>, the coefficient matrices of the state equations and output equations in CCF or OCF, respectively, as those in Equations 7-28 or 7-29 are returned. We next select the `Transformations` to get the DF coefficient matrices given in Equation 7-30. As pointed out in the last section, CCF corresponds to direct decomposition, and DF corresponds to parallel decomposition of a transfer function with distinct poles.

7.6.5 Cascade Decomposition and Series Connection of Systems

Applying the CSAD functions to cascade decomposition requires special attention, because the resulting state representation is not unique. The program `svseries` in CSAD can be used to obtain the equivalent dynamic equations of two SISO systems in state-variable representation connected in series. For the decomposition of a system with more than two subsystems connected in cascade, the program `svseries` can be applied repeatedly.

Figure 7-4 shows the series connection of two systems with the system numbered 1 placed to the right of system 2. This convention is adopted in the program `svsries` because the convention of numbering the state variables x_1, $x_2, \ldots, x_n$, is from right to left on the state diagram.

Let the dynamic equations of the two systems shown in Figure 7-4 be written as

$$\frac{d\mathbf{x}_1(t)}{dt} = \mathbf{A}_1\mathbf{x}_1(t) + \mathbf{B}_1 u_1(t) \qquad (7\text{-}49)$$

where $\mathbf{A}_1$ is $n_1 \times n_1$, and $\mathbf{B}_1$ is $n_1 \times 1$.

$$\frac{d\mathbf{x}_2(t)}{dt} = \mathbf{A}_2\mathbf{x}_2(t) + \mathbf{B}_2 u_2(t) \qquad (7\text{-}50)$$

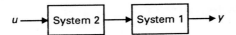

Figure 7-4. Block diagram of two systems connected in cascade.

where $\mathbf{A}_2$ is $n_2 \times n_2$, and $\mathbf{B}_2$ is $n_2 \times 1$.

$$y_1(t) = \mathbf{C}_1 \mathbf{x}_1(t) + D_1 u_1(t) \tag{7-51}$$

$$y_2(t) = \mathbf{C}_2 \mathbf{x}_2(t) + D_2 u_2(t) \tag{7-52}$$

where $\mathbf{C}_1$ is $1 \times n_1$, $\mathbf{C}_2$ is $1 \times n_2$, D_1 and D_2 are scalars.

The state and output equations of the combined system are written

$$\frac{d\mathbf{x}(t)}{dt} = \mathbf{A}\mathbf{x}(t) + \mathbf{B}u(t) \tag{7-53}$$

$$y(t) = \mathbf{C}\mathbf{x}(t) + Du(t) \tag{7-54}$$

From Figure 7-4, $u_2(t) = u(t)$, $u_1(t) = y_2(t)$, and $y(t) = y_1(t)$.

$$\mathbf{x}(t) = \begin{bmatrix} \mathbf{x}_1(t) \\ \mathbf{x}_2(t) \end{bmatrix} \qquad [(n_1 + n_2) \times 1] \tag{7-55}$$

$$\mathbf{A} = \begin{bmatrix} \mathbf{A}_1 & \mathbf{B}_1\mathbf{C}_2 \\ 0 & \mathbf{A}_2 \end{bmatrix} (n_1 + n_2 \times n_1 + n_2) \qquad \mathbf{B} = \begin{bmatrix} \mathbf{B}_1 D_2 \\ \mathbf{B}_2 \end{bmatrix} (n_1 + n_2 \times 1) \tag{7-56}$$

$$\mathbf{C} = [\mathbf{C}_1 \quad D_1\mathbf{C}_2] \ (1 \times n_1 + n_2) \qquad D = D_1 D_2 \ \text{(scalar)}$$

To illustrate the application of `svseries` to cascade decomposition, let us consider the following transfer function, which has three factored components:

$$\frac{Y(s)}{U(s)} = \left(\frac{s+5}{s+2}\right)\left(\frac{2.5}{s+3}\right)\left(\frac{10}{s+10}\right)$$

$$\begin{array}{ccc} \text{System} & \text{System} & \text{System} \\ 1 & 2 & 3 \end{array} \tag{7-57}$$

Because `svseries` handles only two seriesly connected systems, we must first cascade System 1 and System 2 in Equation 7-57, as shown by the state diagram in Figure 7-5. At the MATLAB prompt >>, we enter

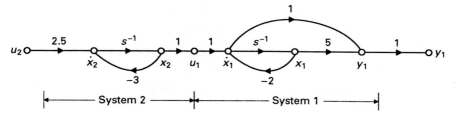

Figure 7-5. Systems 1 and 2 connected in cascade of Equation 7-57.

```
>> a1 = -2 <CR>
>> b1 = 1 <CR>
>> c1 = 3 <CR>
>> d1 = 1 <CR>
>> a2 = -3 <CR>
>> b2 = 2.5 <CR>
>> c2 = 1 <CR>
>> d2 = 0 <CR>
```

Because the two individual systems are decomposed by direct decomposition, the coefficient matrices are in CCF. Then enter [A,B,C,D]=svseries (a1,b1,c1,d1,a2,b2,c2,d2), followed by <CR>, and the program returns

```
A =
        -2      1
         0     -3
B =
         0
        2.5
C =
         3      1
D =
         0
```

Next we connect System 3 in front of the combination of Systems 1 and 2 by entering

```
>> a1 = [-2 1;0 -3] <CR>        These matrices are still available in the
>> b1 = [0;2.5] <CR>           program, so that they do not have to be
>> c1 = [3 1] <CR>             reentered if the matrix variable names
>> d1 = 0 <CR>                 are redesignated.
>> a2 = -10 <CR>
>> b2 = 10 <CR>
>> c2 = 1 <CR>
>> d2 = 0 <CR>
```

Then, again enter [A,B,C,D]=svseries(a1,b1,c1,d1,a2,b2,c2, d2) followed by <CR>, and the following final results are obtained:

```
A =
    -2   1    0
     0  -3   2.5
     0   0  -10
B =
     0
     0
    10
C =
     3   1    0
D =
     0
```

7.6.6 Parallel Connection of Two Systems

Figure 7-6 shows the block diagram of two SISO systems connected in parallel.

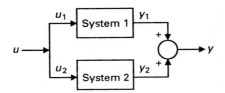

Figure 7-6. Block diagram of two systems connected in parallel.

The dynamic equations of the systems are given in Equations 7-49 to 7-52. The combined system is described by Equations 7-53 and 7-54. From Figure 7-6,

$$u_1(t) = u_2(t) = u(t) \qquad (7\text{-}58)$$

$$y(t) = y_1(t) + y_2(t) \qquad (7\text{-}59)$$

The coefficient matrices of the combined system are

$$\mathbf{A} = \begin{bmatrix} \mathbf{A}_1 & 0 \\ 0 & \mathbf{A}_2 \end{bmatrix} (n_1 + n_2 \times n_1 + n_2) \qquad \mathbf{B} = \begin{bmatrix} \mathbf{B}_1 \\ \mathbf{B}_2 \end{bmatrix} \qquad (7\text{-}60)$$

$$\mathbf{C} = [\mathbf{C}_1 \quad \mathbf{C}_2] \, (1 \times n_1 + n_2) \qquad D = D_1 + D_2 \, (\text{scalar})$$

The CSAD function that performs the parallel connection of two SISO systems in state-variable representation is svparall.

As an illustrative example on the application of svparall, consider that

$$\mathbf{A}_1 = \begin{bmatrix} 1 & -2 \\ 0 & 1 \end{bmatrix} \qquad \mathbf{B}_1 = \begin{bmatrix} 1 \\ -1 \end{bmatrix} \qquad \mathbf{C}_1 = [1 \quad -1] \qquad D_1 = 0$$

Chap. 7   State-Variable Analysis

$$\mathbf{A}_2 = \begin{bmatrix} 0 & 1 \\ -2 & 3 \end{bmatrix} \qquad \mathbf{B}_2 = \begin{bmatrix} 0 \\ 2 \end{bmatrix} \qquad \mathbf{C}_2 = [0 \quad -2] \qquad D_2 = 0$$

To execute `svparall`, we enter the following vectors at the MATLAB prompt >>

```
>> a1 = [1 -2; 0 1] <CR>
>> b1 = [1; -1] <CR>
>> c1 = [1 -1] <CR>
>> d1 = 0 <CR>
>> a2 = [0 1; -2 3] <CR>
>> b2 = [0; 2] <CR>
>> c2 = [0 -2] <CR>
>> d2 = 0 <CR>
```

Then enter `[A,B,C,D,]=svparall(a1,b1,c1,d1,a2,b2,c2,d2)`, followed by <CR>, and the following results are returned:

```
A =
    1   -2    0    0
    0    1    0    0
    0    0    0    1
    0    0   -2    3
B =
    1
   -1
    0
    2
C =
    1   -1    0   -2
D =    0
```

For more than two systems connected in parallel, `svparall` can be applied repeatedly.

7.6.7 Feedback Connections of Two Systems

Figure 7-7 shows the block diagrams of two SISO systems connected in negative feedback form. The dynamic equations of the two subsystems are given in Equations 7-49 to 7-52. The combined system is described by Equations 7-53 and 7-54. From Figure 7-7, $y(t) = y_1(t)$, $u_2(t) = y(t)$, and

$$u_1(t) = u(t) - y_2(t) \tag{7-61}$$

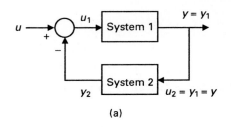

(a)

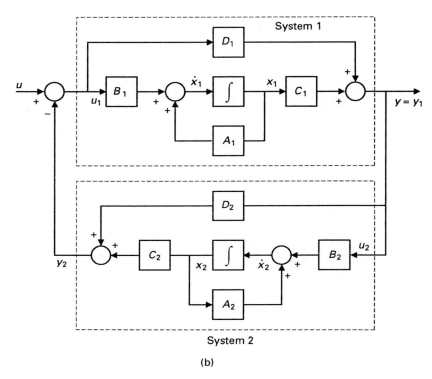

(b)

Figure 7-7. Feedback connection of two systems.

The coefficient matrices of the combined system are

$$\mathbf{A} = \frac{1}{\Delta} \begin{bmatrix} \mathbf{A}_1\Delta - \mathbf{B}_1 D_2 \mathbf{C}_1 & -\mathbf{B}_1 \mathbf{C}_2 \\ \mathbf{B}_2 \mathbf{C}_1 & \mathbf{A}_2\Delta - \mathbf{B}_2 D_1 \mathbf{C}_2 \end{bmatrix} \qquad (7\text{-}62)$$

where

$$\Delta = 1 + D_1 D_2 \quad (\neq 0) \qquad (7\text{-}63)$$

$$\mathbf{B} = \frac{1}{\Delta} \begin{bmatrix} \mathbf{B}_1 \\ \mathbf{B}_2 D_1 \end{bmatrix} \tag{7-64}$$

$$\mathbf{C} = [\mathbf{C}_1 \qquad -D_1 \mathbf{C}_2]/\Delta \tag{7-65}$$

$$D = D_1/\Delta \tag{7-66}$$

svcloop of the *CSAD Toolbox* may be used to perform the feedback connection of two SISO systems. As an illustrative example, consider that the coefficient matrices of two first-order systems are given as

$$A_1 = -2 \qquad B_1 = 1 \qquad C_1 = 1 \qquad D_1 = 1$$

$$A_2 = -3 \qquad B_2 = 1 \qquad C_2 = 1 \qquad D_2 = 1$$

The systems are connected in the form of Figure 7-7.

To apply svcloop, we first enter the coefficient matrices at the MATLAB prompt as:

```
>> a1 = -2 <CR>
>> b1 = 1 <CR>
>> c1 = 1 <CR>
>> d1 = 1 <CR>
>> a2 = -3 <CR>
>> b2 = 1 <CR>
>> c2 = 1 <CR>
>> d2 = 1 <CR>
```

Then, enter [A,B,C,D]=svcloop(a1,b1,c1,d1,a2,b2,c2,d2), followed by <CR>. The returned results are:

```
A =
      -1.5   -0.5
       0.5   -2.0
B =
       0.5
       0.5
C =
       0.5   -0.5
D =
       0.5
```

7.6.8 Feedback System with Constant Feedback

When the system in the feedback path (System 2 in Figure 7-7[a], [b]) is a simple constant gain, *do not* enter $a2 = 0$, $b2 = 0$, $c2 = 0$, and $d2 =$ feedback gain, as this will create an uncontrollable or unobservable composite system. Instead, the proper way to handle this situation is to enter k = feedback gain (note the negative feedback convention used in Figure 7-7), and use the command `[A,B,C,D]=svcloop(a1,b1,c1,d1,k) <CR>`.

7.6.9 Multiple-Loop Systems

The functions `svseries`, `svparall`, and `svcloop` can be applied repeatedly to analyze systems with multiple loops or more complex combined state-variable configurations.

7.7 CONTROLLABILITY AND OBSERVABILITY OF LINEAR TIME-INVARIANT SYSTEMS

The concepts of controllability and observability first introduced by Kalman in 1961 play an important role in the optimal control of linear control systems. The condition on controllability governs the existence of a solution to an optimal control design. For instance, controllability is closely related to the existence of solutions of state feedback for the purpose of placing the eigenvalues of the system arbitrarily. In general, a system is said to be completely controllable if every state variable of the system can be controlled to reach a specific target in finite time by some unconstrained control.

The concept of observability relates to the condition of observing or estimating the state variables that are not accessible (for feedback control) from the output variables, which are generally measurable.

Given the state equations of an nth-order linear time-invariant system as

$$\frac{d\mathbf{x}(t)}{dt} = \mathbf{A}\mathbf{x}(t) + \mathbf{B}\mathbf{u}(t) \tag{7-67}$$

one of the several ways of checking the controllability of the system is that the *controllability matrix*

$$\mathbf{S} = [\mathbf{B} \quad \mathbf{A}\mathbf{B} \quad \mathbf{A}^2\mathbf{B} \quad \mathbf{A}^3\mathbf{B} \quad \cdots \quad \mathbf{A}^{n-1}\mathbf{B}] \tag{7-68}$$

must have a rank of n.

Notice that the controllability matrix $\mathbf{S}$ is identical to the matrix given in Equation 7-14. This indicates that the condition of the existence of CCF is synonymous to the condition of controllability. The only difference is that the CCF is defined here only for single-input systems, whereas controllability applies to systems with any number of inputs.

For observability, we need to include the output equation, in addition to the state equation in Equation 7-67,

$$\mathbf{y}(t) = \mathbf{C}\mathbf{x}(t) + \mathbf{D}\mathbf{u}(t) \tag{7-69}$$

One of the ways of checking on the observability of the system described by Equations 7-67 and 7-69 when $\mathbf{D} = 0$ is that the *observability matrix*

$$V = \begin{bmatrix} C \\ CA \\ CA^2 \\ \vdots \\ CA^{n-1} \end{bmatrix} \qquad (7\text{-}70)$$

must have a rank of n.

Notice that the observability matrix V is identical to the matrix given in Equation 7-24. This indicates that the condition of the existence of OCF is synonymous to the condition of observability.

The function svstuff allows the user to determine the controllability and observability of linear time-invariant systems entered in either the state-variable form or the transfer function (SISO systems) form, after it is transformed to either the CCF or the OCF.

To illustrate the applications of svstuff to controllability and observability, let us enter the coefficient matrices of Equation 7-27 to svstuff. Choosing the Controllability option from the menu, the program returns

```
Controllability Matrix is

    0    0    2
    0    1   -4
    1   -4   13


The System is Controllable.
```

Choosing the Observability option from the menu, the program returns:

```
Observability Matrix is

    1    0    0
   -3    2    0
    7   -6    2


The System is Observable.
```

Now let us enter the transfer function of the system, $2/(s^3 + 7s^2 + 17s + 21)$, using the Input N(s)/D(s) option. The program will first ask whether the CCF or the OCF is to be determined in the state representation.

For the CCF selection, the program returns the **A**, **B**, **C**, **D** matrices as in Equation 7-28, and the results on controllability is

```
Controllability Matrix is

    0    0    1
    0    1   -7
    1   -7   32


The System is Controllable.
```

For observability,

```
Observability Matrix is

    2    0    0
    0    2    0
    0    0    2


The System is Observable.
```

Notice that the controllability and observability matrices obtained here are different from those when the **A**, **B**, **C**, **D** matrices of Equation 7-27 are used, although the results on controllability and observability are the same.

For the OCF selection, the program returns the **A**, **B**, **C**, **D** matrices as in Equation 7-33, and the results on controllability are

```
Controllability Matrix is

    2    0    0
    0    2    0
    0    0    2


The System is Controllable.
```

For observability,

```
Observability Matrix is

    0    0    1
    0    1   -7
    1   -7   32


The System is Observable.
```

It is well known that an input-output transfer function with at least one common pole and zero will result in an uncontrollable or unobservable system, depending on how the state variables are defined. As an illustrative example, let us enter the transfer function

$$\frac{Y(s)}{U(s)} = \frac{s + 1}{(s + 1)(s + 2)} \tag{7-71}$$

which as a common pole and zero at $s = -1$.

Choosing CCF after entering the transfer function, `svstuff` returns,

```
A:
      0   1
     -2  -3
B:
      0
      1
C:
      1   1
D:
      0
Controllability Matrix is:
      0   1
      1  -3
The system is controllable.
Observability Matrix is:
      1   1
     -2  -2
The System is NOT observable. Rank = 1.
```

Choosing OCF after entering the transformation, `svstuff` returns,

```
A:
      0  -1
      1  -3
B:
      1
      1
C:
      0   1
D:
      0
Controllability Matrix is:
      1  -2
      1  -2
The System is NOT controllable. Rank = 1.
Observability Matrix is:
      0   1
      1  -3
The System is observable.
```

Sec. 7.7   Controllability and Observability of Linear Time-Invariant Systems 67

Thus, the system with common pole(s) and zero(s) is modeled as controllable but unobservable in the CCF, and uncontrollable but observable in the OCF.

7.8 UNIT-STEP RESPONSE

svstuff in the *CSAD Toolbox* uses the function svplot to compute and plot the output $y(t)$ of a SISO system with zero initial conditions when the input $u(t)$ is a unit-step function.

After svstuff has been called, the following menu will be displayed.

```
                           - SVSTUFF -

          Eigenvalues        Display A,B,C,D
          Controllability    New A,B,C,D
          Observability      Find N(s)/D(s)
          Transformations    Input N(s)/D(s)
          State feedback     Quit
          Response to step
    Choose Option N or I to Enter a System
    Option? >
```

If the letter I is entered, followed by <CR>, the program will prompt for the data of the matrices **A**, **B**, **C**, and **D**. After the data have been entered, the svstuff menu will reappear, followed by the Option? > prompt. The unit-step response of the system is computed by entering r for "Response to step," followed by <CR>. The svplot options menu will appear on the monitor screen.

```
                       - SVPLOT OPTION -

          Plot            Final time
          Zoom in         New A,B,C,D
          Set axes        Display sys
          Grid plot       Attributes
          Hold plot       Eigenvalues
          Label Plot      View data
                          Quit
```

Selecting "Plot" from the menu will display the unit-step response on the screen.

As an illustrative example, the unit-step response for the following system is obtained as shown in Figure 7-8.

$$\mathbf{A} = \begin{bmatrix} 0 & 1 \\ -10 & -1 \end{bmatrix} \quad \mathbf{B} = \begin{bmatrix} 0 \\ 1 \end{bmatrix} \quad \mathbf{C} = [1 \quad 0] \quad \mathbf{D} = 0 \qquad (7\text{-}72)$$

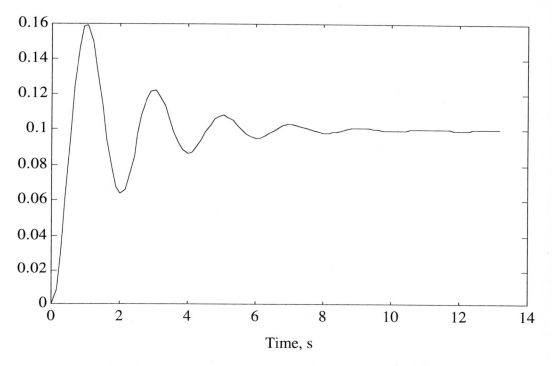

Figure 7-8. Unit-step response of the system described by Equation 7-72.

If the state-feedback design option is first selected, the user is given the choice of finding the unit-step response with or without state feedback using the state-feedback gains computed.

By selecting the `Attributes` option on the `svplot` menu, the following attributes of the step response are displayed:

```
Final value of response is: 1
Delay Time           0.3497
Rise Time            0.3703
Settling Time        5.2
Max % Overshoot      59.4
Time at Max          1.067
```

It must be cautioned that before selecting the `Attributes` *option, it is advisable to first view the step response and see if the time interval and final time are chosen properly by the program, so that all the attributes can be computed accurately. If the step size or the final time is too large you must reset the final time, or the results from the attributes may be in error.* Figure 7-9 shows the initial plot of the following system.

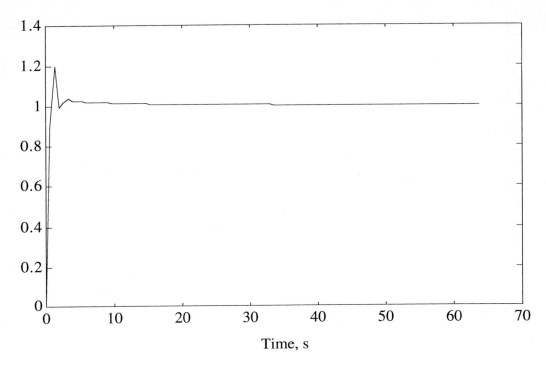

Figure 7-9. Unit-step response of the system described by Equation 7-73.

$$\mathbf{A} = \begin{bmatrix} 0 & 1 & 0 & 0 \\ 0 & 0 & 1 & 0 \\ 0 & 0 & 0 & 1 \\ -15 & -150 & -50 & -15 \end{bmatrix} \quad \mathbf{B} = \begin{bmatrix} 0 \\ 0 \\ 0 \\ 1 \end{bmatrix} \quad (7\text{-}73)$$

$$\mathbf{C} = \begin{bmatrix} 15 & 150 & 0 & 0 \end{bmatrix} \quad \mathbf{D} = 0$$

Notice that the final time is too large and the resolution of the plot is poor. Selecting the `Attributes` gives the following results:

```
Final values of response is: 1
Delay Time              0.3586
Rise Time               0.5759
Settling Time           1.289
Max % Overshoot         20.5
Time at Max             1.289
```

To change the final time of the step response, we select `Final time` and a final time of 10 s. Figure 7-10 shows the plot that has more details of the step response. Now selecting `Attributes` the following results are obtained:

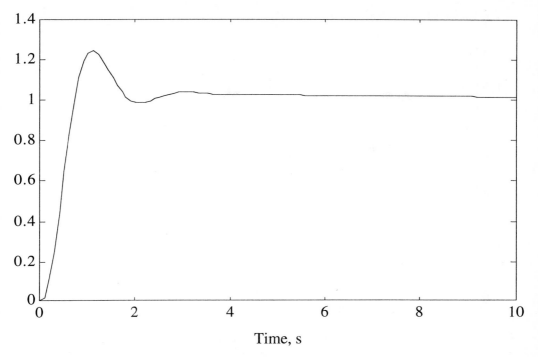

Figure 7-10. Unit-step response of the system described by Equation 7-73. Final time is 10 s.

```
Final value of response is: 1
Delay Time              0.4323
Rise Time               0.4494
Settling Time           1.616
Max % Overshoot         24.5
Time at Max             1.111
```

which are more accurate than those obtained initially.

Plot of multiple runs can be plotted on the same axes if desired. By selecting the Hold plot option of the svplot menu after a plot has been made on the screen, the program will respond by acknowledging

```
Current plot held
```

Then the step response of a second system (or more) can be plotted on the same set of axes by simply entering the system parameters, and executing Plot. Figure 7-11 shows the step response of another slower system superimposed on the step response of Figure 7-10. Again, as pointed out in Chapter 6, once the final time of the first plot is established, the same final time must be set first before plotting all subsequent plots. The scale of vertical axis must be set so that it will contain all the plots.

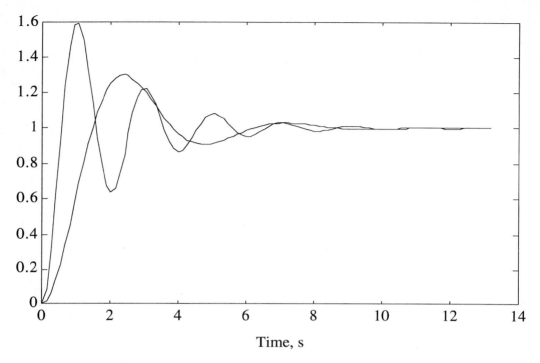

Figure 7-11. Unit-step responses of two systems superposed on one set of axes.

If after calling `svstuff`, the letter *I* is entered at the `Option? >` prompt for `Input N(s)/D(s)`, the program responds by asking for the numerator and denominator polynomials of *N(s)/D(s)*.

```
Default input is: 1
Enter Numerator polynomial > <CR>
Default input is: S^1 + 1
Enter Denominator polynomial> [1  1  10] <CR>
```

which corresponds to the system described by the dynamic equations in Equation 7-72. The program responds by asking

```
Controllable or Observable Form [c] > <CR>
```

For the step response is does not matter whether CCF or OCF is used.

The `svstuff` menu will reappear, and the `Response to step` option may be chosen. The caution on final time and attributes applies again.

The function `svplot` can be run independently, in which case the system can be entered only in the state-variable form.

7.9 IMPULSE AND RAMP RESPONSES

svstuff and svplot do not provide an option for obtaining the unit-impulse and unit-ramp responses of a system. However, these responses can still be obtained by modifying the input-output transfer function $Y(s)/U(s)$. If the system is described by the state-variable responsentation, it is advisable to first find the transfer function using the Find N(s)/D(s) option.

Once the expression of $N(s)/D(s)$ is known, to find the unit-impulse response we simply enter the function $sN(s)/D(s)$. For the unit-ramp response, the function $N(s)/sD(s)$ is entered. See also Section 6.5 on using tftplot.

For the system described by the coefficient matrices in Equation 7-72, we first select Find N(s)/D(s), for which svstuff returns

$$\frac{1}{s^2 + s + 10}$$

Then, select Input N(s)/D(s) by entering i <CR> at the Option? > prompt. The program responds by asking

```
Controllable or Observable Form [c] > <CR>
```

To obtain the impulse response, we multiply the transfer function by s, select the Response to step option, and enter the following data:

```
Default input is: 1
Enter Numerator polynomial> [1  0] <CR>
Default input is: s^1 + 1
Enter Denominator polynomial> [1  1  10]
```

Then, select Response to step by entering r <CR> at the Option? > prompt. The impulse response is plotted as shown in Figure 7-12. To obtain the ramp response, we simply multiply the original transfer function by $1/s$. The following data are entered after selecting the Input N(s)/D(s) option:

```
Enter Numerator polynomial: 1
Enter Denominator polynomial: [1  1  10  0]
```

The ramp response is plotted as shown in Figure 7-13.

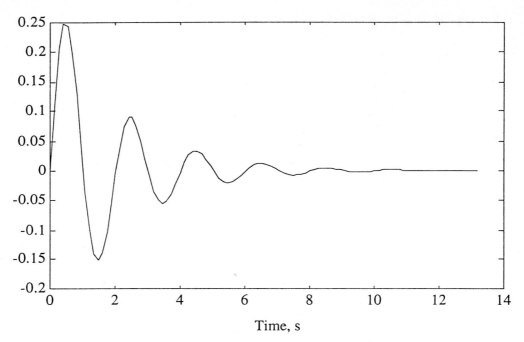

Figure 7-12. Impulse response of the system described by Equation 7-72.

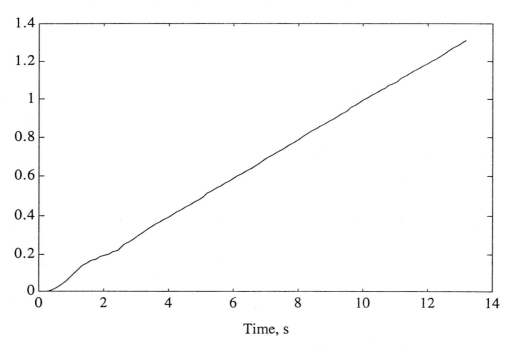

Figure 7-13. Unit-ramp response of the system described by Equation 7-72.

EXERCISES

7-1. Apply the function `svstuff` to find the following items from the following systems described in state-variable form:

(a) Eigenvalues
(b) Controllability
(c) Observability
(d) Transformations to CCF, OCF, and DF
    Skip CCF if the system is uncontrollable.
    Skip OCF if the system is unobservable.
    Skip DF if the system has multiple-order eigenvalues.
(e) Response to a unit-step input
(f) Transfer function $Y(s)/U(s) = N(s)/D(s)$

(i)

$$\mathbf{A} = \begin{bmatrix} -1 & 1 & 0 \\ 0 & -2 & 0 \\ 0 & 0 & -3 \end{bmatrix} \quad \mathbf{B} = \begin{bmatrix} 0 \\ 0 \\ 1 \end{bmatrix} \quad \mathbf{C} = [1 \quad 1 \quad 1] \quad \mathbf{D} = 0$$

(ii)

$$\mathbf{A} = \begin{bmatrix} -3 & 2 & 0 \\ -1 & 0 & 1 \\ -2 & -3 & -4 \end{bmatrix} \quad \mathbf{B} = \begin{bmatrix} 0 \\ 0 \\ 1 \end{bmatrix} \quad \mathbf{C} = [1 \quad 0 \quad 0] \quad \mathbf{D} = 0$$

(iii)

$$\mathbf{A} = \begin{bmatrix} 0 & 1 \\ -1 & -2 \end{bmatrix} \quad \mathbf{B} = \begin{bmatrix} 0 \\ 1 \end{bmatrix} \quad \mathbf{C} = [1 \quad 0] \quad \mathbf{D} = 1$$

7-2. The input-output transfer function of a linear system is given as

$$\frac{Y(s)}{U(s)} = \frac{N(s)}{D(s)} = \frac{s + 2}{s^3 + 6s^2 + 11s + 6}$$

(a) Use the function `svstuff` to decompose the transfer function into CCF. Determine the controllability and observability of the system.
(b) Use the program `svstuff` to decompose the transfer function into OCF. Determine the controllability and observability of the system in OCF.

7-3. The input-output transfer function of a linear system is given as $N(s)/D(s)$.
(a) Use `svstuff` to decompose the transfer function into CCF. Determine the controllability and observability of the system in CCF. Compute and plot the unit-step response.
(b) Repeat part (a) by decomposing the system into OCF.
(c) Repeat part (a) by decomposing the system into DF.

Sec. 7.9   Impulse and Ramp Responses   **75**

(i)

$$\frac{N(s)}{D(s)} = \frac{10(s + 5)}{(s + 1)(s^2 + 5s + 50)}$$

(ii)

$$\frac{N(s)}{D(s)} = \frac{10(s^2 + s + 10)}{(s + 1)(s + 10)(s^2 + s + 1)}$$

7-4. The transfer function of a linear system is factored into subsystems connected in cascade. Find the state-variable representation of the system after expressing the subsystems in CCF. If a state diagram were drawn, the state variables should be numbered from right to left starting with x_1.

(a)

$$\frac{Y(s)}{U(s)} = \left(\frac{s}{s + 50}\right)\left(\frac{5}{s + 5}\right)$$

System   System

1   2

(b)

$$\frac{Y(s)}{U(s)} = \left(\frac{s}{s + 50}\right)\left(\frac{5}{s + 5}\right)\left(\frac{1}{s + 2.5}\right)$$

System   System   System

1   2   3

7-5. Two linear subsystems are connected in parallel as shown in Figure 7P-5. Find the state-variable representation of the system after expressing the subsystems in CCF.

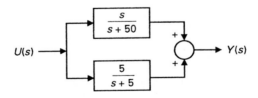

Figure 7P-5.

7-6. Two linear subsystems are connected in a feedback configuration as shown in Figure 7P-6. Find the state-variable representation of the system after expressing the subsystems in OCF.

7-7. Apply the functions `svseries` and `svcloop` repeatedly to find the dynamic equations of the system shown in Figure 7P-7. First decompose the subsystems in each block into CCF using `svstuff`. Number the state variables x_1, x_2, and x_3 according to Systems 1, 2, and 3, respectively.

Chap. 7   State-Variable Analysis

Answer:

A =

```
    0    5    0
   -5  -10    1
    0    5   -2
```

B =

```
    0
    1
    0
```

C =

```
    1    0    0
```

D =

```
    0
```

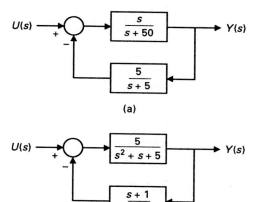

(a)

(b)

Figure 7P-6.

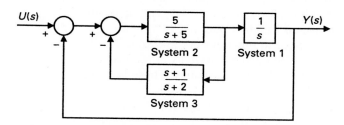

Figure 7P-7.

Time-Domain Analysis

8.1 INTRODUCTION

A realistic way of evaluating the performance of a control system is to study its response in the time domain when test signals such as step function, ramp function, or parabolic function are applied.

The time response of a control system can be divided into two parts: the transient response and the steady-state response. Transient response is defined as the part of the response that goes to zero as time approaches infinity. The steady-state response is the part of the total response that remains after the transient has died out.

Several functions in the *CSAD Toolbox* can be used to analyze and design linear SISO control systems in the time domain, or rather, with respect to the time-domain characteristics. These functions are

`routh`   Produces the Routh tabulation for stability studies.

`tftplot`   Computes unit-step response from input-output transfer function. Gives attributes of the transient response and the final value of the steady-state response. Can be used for ramp and parabolic inputs.

`svplot`   Computes unit-step response from dynamic equations. Gives attributes of the transient response and the final value of the steady-state response.

78

`svstuff`	Options menu of this program contains `tftplot` and `svplot`.
`iltplot`	Computes the inverse Laplace transform of a proper transfer function. This program can be used to evaluate the output of a linear system with any input that can be represented as a Laplace transform.
`svord2`	Find the state variable description of a second-order system given a desired damping ratio ζ, and an undamped natural frequency ω_n.
`tfess`	Evaluates the error constants and the steady-state errors of single-loop systems with step input, ramp input, and parabolic input, using the loop transfer function $G(s)H(s)$.
`rlplot`	Generates root locus plots in the s-plane.
`tford2`	Generates the prototype second-order system transfer function from transient characteristics.

8.2 STABILITY OF LINEAR SISO SYSTEMS

It is defined in the literature that a linear time-invariant SISO system is stable if its output is bounded to a bounded input. If this condition is not satisfied, the system is unstable. The stability condition can be investigated by simply checking on the roots of the characteristic equation. The roots of the characteristic equation of a stable system must all be located in the left half of the s-plane. When the characteristic equation has at least one simple root on the $j\omega$-axis and none in the right half of the s-plane, the system is said to be marginally stable or marginally unstable. If the characteristic equation has multiple-order roots on the $j\omega$-axis or at least one root in the right-half s-plane, it is unstable.

Given the characteristic equation of a linear SISO system, the roots of the equation can be computed using `roots` in the MATLAB *Toolbox*. The function `routh` of the *CSAD Toolbox* can be used to obtain the Routh's tabulation to indicate the number of roots of the equation that are in the right-half s-plane. Because the `roots` gives the exact location of the roots, the use of `routh` is perhaps academic. The true value of the Routh criterion is in determining the location of the roots, with respect to the left- and right-half s-plane, of a characteristic equation with one or more variable parameters. The function `routh` is useful only for polynomials with known coefficients and is included here only for completeness. The applications of `roots` and `routh` are illustrated by the following examples.

Consider that the characteristic equation is

$$s^3 + 2s^2 + 3s + 4 = 0 \qquad (8\text{-}1)$$

The polynomial vector is entered at the MATLAB prompt.

```
>> c=1 2 3 4; <CR>
>> roots(c) <CR>
ans =
    -1.6506
    -0.1747 + 1.5469i
    -0.1747 - 1.5469i
```

The Routh tabulation is obtained by executing `routh` at the MATLAB prompt, using the same polynomial.

```
>> routh(c) <CR>
s^3 Row:
     1  3
s^2 Row:
     2  4
s^1 Row:
     1  0
s^0 Row:
     4
Press any key to continue
First Column is:
       s^3  1
       s^2  2
       s^1  1
       s^0  4
Number of sign changes in the first column is 0.
```

As another example, consider the equation

$$s^4 + s^3 + s^2 + s + 1 = 0 \qquad\qquad (8\text{-}2)$$

The polynomial vector is entered at the MATLAB prompt,

```
>> c=[1 1 1 1 1];
>> roots(c)
ans =
     0.3090 + 0.9511i
     0.3090 - 0.9511i
    -0.8090 + 0.5878i
    -0.8090 - 0.5878i
```

For the Routh criterion,

```
>> routh(c)
s^4 Row:
     1  1  1
s^3
     1  1  0
Zero element in first column of the next row
Replacing zero with 1e - 5
s^2 Row:
     1.0000e - 005  1.0000e + 000  0
s^1 Row:
    -99999              0
s^0 Row:
     1
```

```
Press any key to continue
First column is:
    s^4   1
    s^3   1
    s^2   1e - 005
    s^1   -1e + 005
    s^0   1
Number of sign changes in the first column is 2.
```

Several other programs of CSAD can also be used to determine the stability of a linear SISO system by finding the roots of the characteristic equation or the eigenvalues of the system. If the system is described by the coefficient matrices **A**, **B**, **C**, and **D**, the programs svstuff and svplot can be used to find the eigenvalues of the system. If the transfer function of the system is given, then the programs svstuff and tftplot can be used to find the poles of the transfer function. In svstuff the transfer function is first transformed into either CCF or OCF, and then choose the eigenvalues of the OPTIONS MENU. For the tftplot, selecting the roots option gives the zeros and the poles of the transfer function.

8.3 STEADY-STATE PERFORMANCE

The steady-state performance of a stable linear control system can be measured by defining the *steady-state error* e_{ss}. Consider the linear SISO system shown in Figure 8-1. The error of the system is defined as

$$e(t) = r(t) - b(t) \tag{8-3}$$

The steady-state error of the system is defined as

$$e_{ss} = \lim_{t \to \infty} e(t) \tag{8-4}$$

Applying the final-value theorem of Laplace transform to e_{ss} for the system in Figure 8-1, the steady-state error is written

$$e_{ss} = \lim_{s \to \infty} \frac{sR(s)}{1 + G(s)H(s)} \tag{8-5}$$

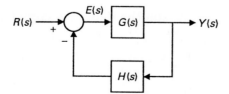

Figure 8-1. Linear single-loop control system.

8.3.1 The Type of Control Systems

Equation 8-5 indicates that the steady-state error of the system in Figure 8-1 depends on the loop transfer function $G(s)H(s)$ and the input $R(s)$. The steady-state error can be more easily computed if the system is classified according to the form of $G(s)H(s)$. In general, $G(s)H(s)$ can be expressed as

$$G(s)H(s) = \frac{K(1 + T_1 s)(1 + T_2 s) \cdots (1 + T_m s)}{s^j (1 + T_a s)(1 + T_b s) \cdots (1 + T_n s)} e^{-T_d s} \qquad (8\text{-}6)$$

where K and all the T's are real constants. The *type* of the closed-loop system refers to the order of the pole of $G(s)H(s)$ at $s = 0$. Therefore, the closed-loop system that has $G(s)H(s)$ described by Equation 8-6 is type j, where $j = 0, 1, 2, \ldots$. The other factors and the coefficients of $G(s)H(s)$ are not important to the system type. The following examples on system type with reference to the form of $G(s)H(s)$ are given.

$$G(s)H(s) = \frac{K(s + 5)}{s(s + 1)(s + 2)} \qquad \text{type } 1 \qquad (8\text{-}7)$$

$$G(s)H(s) = \frac{K}{s^2(s + 12)} \qquad \text{type } 2 \qquad (8\text{-}8)$$

8.3.2 The Error Constants

To facilitate the study of steady-state errors of linear systems, *error constants* are defined for step input, ramp input, and parabolic inputs. The error constants for the three types of inputs and their relationships to the steady-state error are summarized as follows.

Step-Error Constant K_p and the Step-Function Input

When the system in Figure 8-1 is subject to a step input of magnitude R, the step-error constant is defined as

$$\text{Step-error constant } K_p = \lim_{s \to 0} G(s)H(s) \qquad (8\text{-}9)$$

The steady-state error is given by

$$\text{Steady-state error } e_{ss} = \frac{R}{1 + K_p} \qquad (8\text{-}10)$$

Ramp-Error Constant K_v and the Ramp-Function Input

When the system in Figure 8-1 is subject to a ramp input of magnitude R, that is, $r(t) = R t u_s(t)$, where $u_s(t)$ is the unit-step function, the ramp-error constant is defined as

$$K_v = \lim_{s \to 0} s G(s)H(s) \qquad (8\text{-}11)$$

The steady-state error is given by

$$e_{ss} = \frac{R}{K_v} \qquad (8\text{-}12)$$

Parabolic-Error Constant K_a and the Parabolic-Function Input

When the system in Figure 8-1 is subject to a parabolic input, $r(t) = Rt^2 u_s(t)/2$, the parabolic-error constant is defined as

$$K_a = \lim_{s \to 0} s^2 G(s)H(s) \qquad (8\text{-}13)$$

The steady-state error is given by

$$e_{ss} = \frac{R}{K_a} \qquad (8\text{-}14)$$

It must be pointed out that the error constants and steady-state analysis is meaningful only if the system is stable. In other words, the roots of the characteristic equation must all be in the left half of the s-plane.

The function tfess of the *CSAD Toolbox* evaluates the error constants, K_p, K_v, and K_a, and the corresponding steady-state errors owing to the step, ramp, and parabolic inputs, respectively. The numerator and denominator polynomials of the loop-transfer function $G(s)H(s)$ are entered as inputs to the program. As an illustrative example, consider that

$$G(s)H(s) = \frac{100}{s(s^2 + 10s + 100)} \qquad (8\text{-}15)$$

The characteristic equation of the closed-loop system is obtained by adding the numerator polynomial to the denominator polynomial.

$$s^3 + 10s^2 + 100s + 100 = 0 \qquad (8\text{-}16)$$

For more complex functions, we can use the program padd to add the two polynomials. Applying the program roots to Equation 8-16, the roots of the characteristic equation are found.

$$-4.4453 + 8.389i$$
$$-4.4453 - 8.389i$$
$$-1.1094$$

The closed-loop system is stable, because the three roots of the characteristic equation are all in the left-half s-plane. We start the function tfess by entering tfess at the MATLAB prompt.

Sec. 8.3   Steady-State Performance   **83**

```
>> tfess <CR>
Enter Numerator Polynomial > 100; <CR>
Enter Denominator Polynomial > pmult([1 0],[1 10 100]); <CR>
This system is type 1
Step error constant, Kp        inf
Unit step Ess                   0
Ramp Error constant, Kv         1
Unit Ramp Ess                   1
Parabolic Error constant, Ka    0
(t^2)/2 parabolic Ess          inf
```

Consider the loop transfer function,

$$G(s)H(s) = \frac{100}{s^2(s^2 + 10s + 100)} \qquad (8\text{-}17)$$

The characteristic equation of the closed-loop system is

$$s^4 + 10s^3 + 100s^2 + 100 = 0 \qquad (8\text{-}18)$$

The roots are

$$-5.0505 + 8.6321i$$
$$-5.0505 - 8.6321i$$
$$0.0505 + 0.9986i$$
$$0.0505 - 0.9986i$$

Because there are two roots in the right-half s-plane, the closed-loop system is unstable. Therefore, it would be meaningless to run the `tfess` program.

8.4 TRANSIENT RESPONSE

The transient response of a stable linear system represents the portion of the response before the steady state is reached. For a stable system, the transient response gives a measure of the degree of stability or *relative stability* of the system.

8.4.1 The Unit-Step Response and Time-Domain Specifications

The transient performance of a stable linear control system is often measured by using the output from a unit-step function input, the *unit-step response*. Figure 8-2 illustrates a typical unit-step response with zero steady-state error. The performance criteria commonly used for the characterization of the unit-step response of a linear control system are given as follows:

1. *Maximum overshoot.* Let $y(t)$ be the unit-step response, y_{max} be the maximum value of $y(t)$, y_{ss} be the steady-state value of $y(t)$, (which may not be equal to unity), and $y_{max} \geq y_{ss}$. The maximum overshoot of $y(t)$ is defined as

$$\text{maximum overshoot} = y_{max} - y_{ss} \qquad (8\text{-}19)$$

The maximum overshoot is often represented as a percentage of the final value of the step response; that is,

$$\text{percent maximum overshoot} = \frac{\text{maximum overshoot}}{y_{ss}} \times 100\% \qquad (8.20)$$

2. *Delay time.* The delay time t_d is defined as the time required for step response to reach 50% of its final value (see Figure 8-2).

3. *Rise time.* The rise time t_r is defined as the time required for the step response to rise from 10% to 90% of its final value (see Figure 8-2).

4. *Settling time.* The settling time t_s is the time required for the step response to decrease and stay within 5% of its final value (see Figure 8-2).

The functions, `svstuff`, `tftplot`, `svplot`, and `tddesign` in the CSAD toolbox contain unit-step response capabilities that provide computation on these four transient characteristics from the `attributes` option. The use of `tftplot`, `svplot`, and `svstuff` to compute the step responses has been described in Sections 6.5 and 7.8.

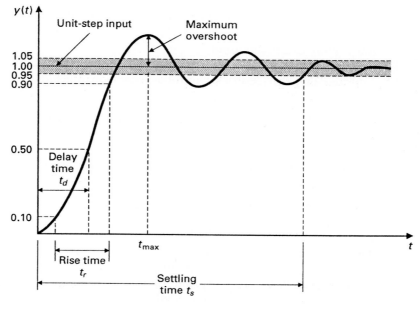

Figure 8-2. Typical unit-step response.

For example, the attributes of the system with the input-output transfer function given in Equation 6-28 are computed to be

```
Final value of response is: 1
Delay time           0.3497
Rise time            0.3703
Settling time        5.2
Max % overshoot      59.4
Time at max          1.067
```

The unit-step response of the system is shown in Figure 6-3.

As mentioned in Chapter 6, the step size and final time of the unit-step response in the CSAD functions are determined internally by the program, depending on the time constants of the system. *Occasionally, the step size or final time of the simulation may be too large, and the correct attributes of the step response may be distorted by the lack of data points in the vital portion of the response. You should always view the step response before calling the* attri- butes *option, to see if the attributes are adequately represented by the response shown; otherwise, choose a smaller final time.*

8.5 FIRST- AND SECOND-ORDER SYSTEMS

Few practical control systems in the real world are simple enough to be described by first- or second-order transfer functions. However, characteristics of these low-order systems give insight to the behavior of higher-order systems.

8.5.1 First-Order Systems

Consider that the feedback control system shown in Figure 8-1 has the open-loop transfer function

$$G(s) = \frac{1}{Ts} \qquad (8-21)$$

where T is a real constant. The feedback transfer function $H(s)$ is unity. The closed-loop transfer function of the overall system is

$$\frac{Y(s)}{R(s)} = \frac{1}{1 + Ts} = \frac{1/T}{s + 1/T} \qquad (8-22)$$

The unit-step responses of the system are computed using tftplot for $T = $ 0.25, 0.5, 1, 2, and 3, and are plotted as shown in Figure 8-3. The final values of all the responses are unity, and there is no overshoot. The other attributes of the step responses are given as follows:

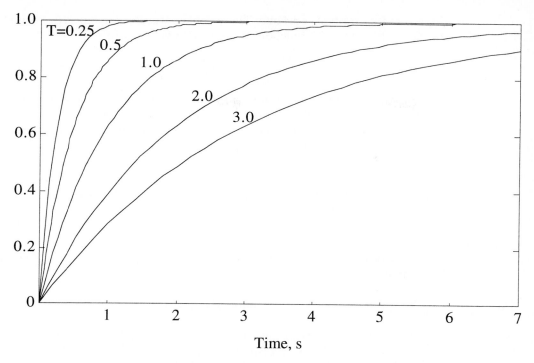

Figure 8-3. Unit-step responses of $1/(1 + Ts)$ for $T = 0.25, 0.5, 1.0, 2.0,$ and $3.0.$

T	3	2	1	0.5	0.25
Delay time (s)	2.081	1.387	0.6937	0.3468	0.1734
Rise time (s)	6.592	4.394	2.197	1.099	0.5493
Settling time (s)	8.8	5.867	2.933	1.467	0.7333

From these attributes we see that as the value of T increases, the delay time, rise time, and settling time of the step response all increase. For the first-order system of Equation 8-22, T is also known as the *time constant* of the system, which is defined as *the time for the step response to reach to 63.2% of its final value*. This illustrative example also shows that the step response of a stable first-order system will never exhibit an overshoot.

8.5.2 Second-Order Systems

Consider that the open-loop transfer function of the system shown in Figure 8-1 is of the form

$$G(s) = \frac{\omega_n^2}{s(s + 2\zeta\omega_n)} \tag{8-23}$$

where ζ and ω_n are real constants. The feedback transfer function $H(s)$ is unity. The closed-loop transfer function of the system is

$$\frac{Y(s)}{R(s)} = \frac{\omega_n^2}{s^2 + 2\zeta\omega_n s + \omega_n^2} \tag{8-24}$$

A second-order closed-loop system with the transfer functions given by Equations 8-23 and 8-24 is called a *prototype second-order system*.

The characteristic equation of the prototype second-order system is obtained by setting the denominator of Equation 8-24 to zero.

$$s^2 + 2\zeta\omega_n s + \omega_n^2 = 0 \tag{8-25}$$

For a unit-step input, the output transform $Y(s)$ is written

$$Y(s) = \frac{\omega_n^2}{s(s^2 + 2\zeta\omega_n s + \omega_n^2)} \tag{8-26}$$

Taking the inverse Laplace on both sides of the last equation, we have the unit-step response,

$$y(t) = 1 - \frac{e^{-\zeta\omega_n t}}{\sqrt{1 - \zeta^2}} \sin(\omega_n\sqrt{1 - \zeta^2}\, t + \cos^{-1}\zeta)\ (t \geq 0) \tag{8-27}$$

When the two roots of the characteristic equation are real and negative, the system is stable. The step response of the system will not exhibit any overshoot and will be similar to those shown in Figure 8-3.

When the two roots of the characteristic equation are complex, the second part of Equation 8-27 will be a damped sinusoid, decaying with increasing time if the system is stable.

The roots of Equation 8-26 are

$$s_1, s_2 = -\zeta\omega_n \pm j\omega_n\sqrt{1 - \zeta^2} \tag{8-28}$$

Figure 8-4 shows the location of the two roots as a complex-conjugate pair. The real part of the roots is $-\zeta\omega_n$, whereas the distance from the origin to the roots is ω_n. The maximum overshoot of the unit-step response can be determined by working with Equation 8-27, and the result is

$$\text{maximum overshoot} = y_{max} - 1 = e^{\frac{-\pi\zeta}{\sqrt{1-\zeta^2}}} \tag{8-29}$$

Thus, we see that the maximum overshoot of the unit-step function of the prototype second-order system is dependent on the value of ζ only. The time at which the maximum overshoot occurs is given by

$$t_{max} = \frac{\pi}{\omega_n\sqrt{1 - \zeta^2}} \tag{8-30}$$

which depends on both ζ and ω_n.

Because ζ governs the value of the maximum overshoot, it governs the damping of the step response; it is defined as the *damping ratio*. As shown in

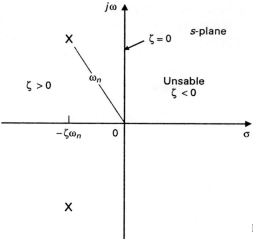

Figure 8-4. Relationship between the characteristic system, and ζ and ω_n.

Figure 8-4, when $\zeta = 0$, the two roots lie on the $j\omega$-axis in the s-plane. The corresponding step response is a pure sinusoid with frequency ω_n. Thus, ω_n is defined as the *undamped natural frequency*.

To illustrate the significance of the damping ratio ζ, Figure 8-5 shows the unit-step response of the prototype second-order system with several positive

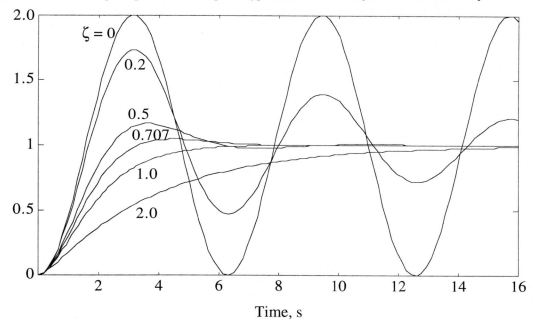

Figure 8-5. Unit-step responses of prototype second-order system with $\omega_n = 1$ and $\zeta = 0, 0.2, 0.5,$ 0.707, 1.0, and 2.0.

Sec. 8.5   First- and Second-Order Systems

values of ζ, and $\omega_n = 1$ rd/s. Notice that as the value of ζ decreases, the maximum overshoot increases. The response also becomes more oscillatory. When $\zeta \geq 1$, the maximum overshoot becomes zero. *Critical damping* refers to the condition when $\zeta = 1$. As ζ decreases, the response also becomes more oscillatory. Eventually, when $\zeta = 0$, zero damping, the system is marginally stable, the step response becomes a pure sinusoid. When ζ is negative, the system is unstable, and the response will increase without bound.

The attributes of the step responses when the system is stable are tabulated as follows:

Damping ratio ζ	0.2	0.5	0.707	1	2
Delay time (s)	1.13	1.294	1.433	1.678	2.867
Rise time (s)	1.226	1.641	2.149	3.358	8.232
Settling time (s)	13.67	5.2	2.923	4.733	11.44
% Max overshoot	52.2	16.3	4.3	0	0
t_{max} (s)	3.333	3.6	4.432	6.6	24.63

The final value is 1 for all values of $\zeta \geq 0$.

These attributes show that when ζ increases delay time and rise time all increase. The settling time is large for small and large values of ζ. The maximum overshoot decreases as ζ increases, but at the expense of delay time, rise time, and settling time. For these reasons, in the classical design the optimum value for ζ is often selected to be 0.707, because it gives a maximum overshoot of only 4.3%, and yet the delay, rise, and settling times are all reasonable.

Next we fix the value of ζ and investigate the effects of varying ω_n. Setting $\zeta = 0.5$ in Equation 8-24, the step responses of the prototype second-order system are plotted in Figure 8-6 for several values of ω_n. Because the value of ζ is constant, the maximum overshoot does not vary with ω_n. The attributes of the responses are tabulated below.

ω_n (rd/sec)	5	10	20
Delay time (s)	0.2588	0.1294	0.06471
Rise time (s)	0.3282	0.1641	0.08205
Settling time	1.04	0.52	0.26
% Max overshoot	16.3	16.3	16.3
t_{max} (s)	0.72	0.36	0.18

These results show that as the value of ω_n increases the values of delay time, rise time, settling time, and t_{max} all decrease, and the maximum overshoot stays constant. Thus, in the classical design of control systems, the designer often calls for a high natural undamped frequency to produce a response that rises and settles fast, without penalizing the overshoot. However, from a practical standpoint a high ω_n requires a high loop gain that can be costly and cause instability in high-order systems.

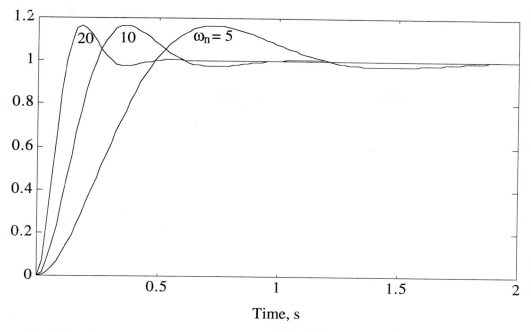

Figure 8-6. Unit-step responses of prototype second-order system with $\zeta = 0.5$ and $\omega_n = 5$, 10, and 20 rd/s.

8.5.3 Analytical Expressions for t_r and t_s

Analytical expressions are more difficult to determine for rise time and settling time, even for just the prototype second-order system. The following approximation formulas are established for t_r and t_s using the damping ratio ζ and natural-undamped frequency ω_n of the prototype second-order system. These equations can be applied to high-order systems that have a pair of dominant poles characterized by ζ and ω_n.

$$t_r \cong \frac{1 - 0.4167\zeta + 2.917\zeta^2}{\omega_n} \qquad 0 < \zeta < 1 \qquad (8\text{-}31)$$

$$t_s \cong \frac{2\zeta^2 + 3}{\zeta\omega_n} \qquad 0 < \zeta < 1 \qquad (8\text{-}32)$$

These equations are useful when maximum values of the maximum overshoot, t_r and t_s are given in design, and the corresponding bounds on ζ and ω_n are desired. Given the maximum bound on y_{max}, the minimum value of ζ is determined from Equation 8-29. The minimum value of ω_n is determined from Equation 8-31 or Equation 8-32, depending on whether the maximum value of t_r or t_s is specified. If the maximum values of t_r and t_s are both specified, the minimum value of ω_n is determined as the largest value from Equations 8-31 and 8-32.

The approximating equations for t_r and t_s as well as Equation 8-29 are used as guidelines for time-domain design in the CSAD function `tddesign`.

8.5.4 `tford2`

The function `tford2` in the *CSAD Toolbox* is designed to find the transfer function of the prototype second-order system in Equation 8-24 given the values of ζ and ω_n.

8.5.5 Closed-Loop Systems Simulation

It should be pointed out that the CSAD functions, `svplot`, `tftplot`, `svstuff` and `iltplot` all depend on the input data between the input and output of an SISO system, whether the system is represented in state-variable or transfer function form. When a system has feedback loop or loops, the closed-loop transfer function of the system must first be determined, or the transfer function can be entered by using the `polyadd`, `pmult`, and `tfcloop` functions.

For time-domain analysis of closed-loop systems it is more convenient to use `tddesign`, although it is intended for PID-controller design. With the `tddesign`, the closed-loop system performance of a single-loop system with unity feedback may be analyzed by entering the open-loop transfer function and setting $K_p = 1$, $K_d = 0$, and $K_i = 0$. The options menu of `tddesign` is shown below.

```
-TDDESIGN OPTIONS-

Controller values
Root locus
Step Response
Goals to meet
Error, steady state
Display TF's
Poles and Zeros
New Plant TF
Quit
```

By choosing the `Step Response` option from the `tddesign`'s menu, the function automatically calls `tftplot`, which computes the step response of the output $y(t)$ or the error signal $e(t)$ of the closed-loop system. Entering `Quit` will get you back to the `tddesign` menu. Choosing `Root locus` from the `tddesign` will lead to `rlplot` and all its capabilities. The `Error, steady state` option gives the steady-state errors of the closed-loop system with unit-step and unit-ramp inputs. More descriptions on how to use `tddesign` will be given in Chapter 10.

8.6 ROOT-LOCUS DIAGRAM

One of the most popular methods of classical analysis and design of linear control systems is the *root-locus plot*. A root-locus plot represents the trajectories of the roots of the characteristic equation when a constant parameter varies. The function `rlplot` in the *CSAD Toolbox* computes and plots the root loci of a linear control system with rational transfer functions. The transfer function is of the form, $K \times N(s)/D(s)$, where K is a real constant, that can lie between $-\infty$ and ∞; $N(s)$ and $D(s)$ are polynomials with real coefficients. The root loci represent the trajectories of roots of the characteristic equation that satisfy the equation

$$1 + \frac{KN(s)}{D(s)} = 0 \tag{8-33}$$

The properties and rules of construction of root loci are given in standard texts on control systems. To help with the understanding of the outputs of the program `rlplot`, the properties of root loci are summarized in the following.

8.6.1 Properties of the Root Loci

$K = 0$ Points: The $K = 0$ points are the poles of $N(s)/D(s)$, or the zeros of $D(s)$, counting the ones at $s = \infty$.

$K = \pm\infty$ Points: The $K = \infty$ points are the zeros of $N(s)/D(s)$, or the zeros of $N(s)$, counting the ones at $s = \infty$.

Asymptotes of the Root Loci: The asymptotes of the root loci describe the properties of the root loci when $|s|$ approaches infinity. The asymptotes are characterized by the angles and their intersect which is always on the real axis.
The angles of the asymptotes are given by the following:
For $K > 0$,

$$\theta_k = \frac{(2k + 1)\pi}{|n - m|} \qquad n \neq m \tag{8-34}$$

where n is the order of $N(s)$ and m is the order of $D(s)$; $k = 0, 1, 2, \ldots,$ $|n - m| - 1$.
For $K < 0$,

$$\theta_k = \frac{2k\pi}{|n - m|} \qquad n \neq m \tag{8-35}$$

where $k = 0, 1, 2, \ldots, |n - m| - 1$. When $n = m$, the root loci do not have any asymptotes.

Root Loci on the Real Axis: The entire real axis of the s-plane is occupied by either the $K \geq 0$ loci or the $K \leq 0$ loci.

Angles of Departure of the Root Loci: The angle of departure of a root locus at a pole or zero of $N(s)/D(s)$ denotes the angle of the tangent to the locus near the point. Strictly, the angle at a zero should be called the *angle of arrival*.

Breakaway Points: Breakaway points on the root loci correspond to multiple-order roots. The breakaway points must satisfy the following equation:

$$\frac{dN(s)}{dD(s)} = 0 \tag{8-36}$$

It is important to note that not all the solutions of the last equation are breakaway points on the root loci. The function `rlplot` gives all the solutions to Equation 8-36. It is fairly easy to select the true breakaway points from the possible ones once the root locus plot is examined.

Intersection of the Root Loci with the Imaginary Axis: The points (if any) where the root loci intersect the imaginary axis of the *s*-plane represent the condition of marginal stability. The function `rlplot` provides an option to find the value of K at any point on the root loci. The function will compute the value of K at the designated point on the loci, as well as all the roots with the same value of K. A mouse is best suited for this purpose. For MS-DOS computers that are not equipped with a mouse, the arrows on the numbers pad may be used, but the resolution is poor.

The Constant ζ Line and the ω_n Circle: The options menu of `rlplot` allows the placement of a constant-ζ line or a constant-ω_n circle in the *s*-plane. The value of K and the corresponding roots at the intersect with any of these trajectory may be best determined by the use of a mouse.

The following example illustrates the application of `rlplot` to the construction of root locus plots:

Consider the transfer function

$$\frac{KN(s)}{D(s)} = \frac{K(s + 3)}{s(s + 5)(s + 6)(s^2 + 2s + 2)} \tag{8-37}$$

which has zeros at $s = -3, \infty, \infty, \infty, \infty$, and poles at $s = 0, -5, -6, -1 + j1$, and $-1 - j1$.

To execute `rlplot`, we type the name of the function at the MATLAB prompt.

```
>> rlplot <CR>
Default input is: s^1 + 3
Enter Numerator Polynomial > [1 3] <CR>
Default input is: s^2 + 2s^1 + 2
Enter Denominator Polynomial > Pmult([1 0],[1 5],[1 6],[1 2 2]) <CR>
```

The pole-zero configuration of $N(s)/D(s)$ will be displayed on the monitor screen, as shown in Figure 8-7.

The following options menu will appear:

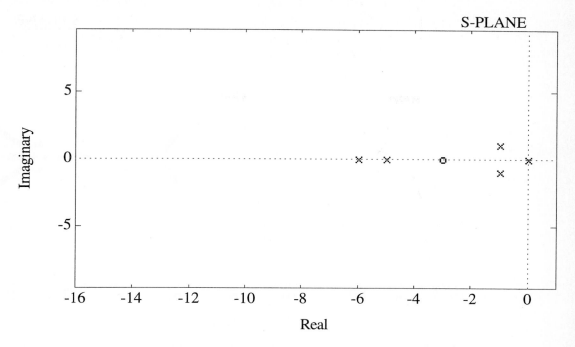

Figure 8-7. Pole-zero configuration of $G(s) = \dfrac{K(s + 3)}{s(s + 5)(s + 6)(s^2 + 2s + 2)}$.

```
                  -RLPLOT OPTIONS-
              K values       Zeta line
              Single K       Wn circle
              Find K         Rule info
              Marginal K     New/clear
              Grid           Display TF
              Title          Quit
   Option? >k <CR>    (Select K values to plot root loci.)
   Enter k values to plot >linspace(0,400) <CR>
```

This command will give a root locus at 100 (default) linearly spaced points starting at $K = 0$ and ending at $K = 400$. Using `linspace(-100,400,50)` gives 50 linearly spaced points from $K = -100$ to $K = 400$. A logarithmically spaced plot for K can also be done by using, for example, `logspace(-1, 2, 100)` computes 100 logarithmically spaced points from $K = 0.1$ to $K = 100$. Other options are described in the *CSAD Toolbox* Reference section on `rlplot`.

The root locus plot is shown in Figure 8-8 for the range of K and number of points specified. The right-half plane of the root-locus axis is limited, because most of the important information for analysis and design lies in the left-half

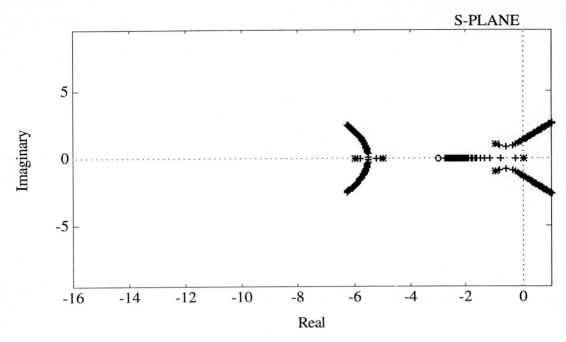

Figure 8-8. Root locus plot of Equation 8-37 for $K = 0$ to $K = 400$ with linear spacing of 100 points.

plane. With a color monitor, the $K > 0$ loci are plotted in red, and the $K < 0$ loci are in green.

Selecting the `Rule info` option from the menu, we get the following information:

```
K = 0 points                    K = inf points
0                               -3.0000e + 00
-6.0000e + 000                  ∞
-5.0000e + 000                  ∞
-1.0000e + 000 + 1.0000e + 000i ∞
-1.0000e + 000 - 1.0000e + 000i ∞
Asymptote angles in degrees for
     K > 0      K < 0
      45          0
     135         90
     225        180
     315        270
Asymptote intersection is: -2.5
Press any key to continue . . .
K > 0 root loci appears on the real axis between:
0 and -3
-5 and -6
K < 0 root loci appears along all
```

```
other sections of the real axis.
Angles of departure for K > 0 are
     Pole                                              Angle (deg)
     -1.0000e + 000 - 1.0000e + 000i                   4.3781e + 001
     -1.0000e + 000 + 1.0000e + 000i                  -4.3781e + 001
Possible Breakaway Points, and associated |K| values are:
             Point                                       |K|
     -5.5257e + 000                                    1.1718e + 001
     -3.3311e + 000 + 1.2040e + 001i                  1.2830e + 002
     -3.3311e + 000 - 1.2040e + 001i                  1.2830e + 002
     -6.5604e - 001 + 4.6768e - 001i                  7.5478e + 000
     -6.5604e - 001 - 4.6768e - 001i                  7.5478e + 000
jω-axis crossing can be found by using Find K option
```

Investigating the root locus plot in Figure 8-8, we see that the only break-away point for all positive and negative values of K is at -5.5257 ($K = 11.718$). The four complex solutions are not breakaway points, although in general break-away points can be complex-conjugate numbers. The values of $|K|$ associated with these false solutions are meaningless.

Let us next select the Zeta line option.

```
Option? >z <CR>
Enter desired damping ratio: zeta > 0.5
```

Because for $K > 0$ the root loci that represent the dominant roots lie only to the right of the poles of $N(s)/D(s)$ at $-1 \pm j1$, it is inappropriate to select a damping ratio ζ greater than or equal to 0.707. The root locus plot with the $\zeta = 0.5$ line is shown in Figure 8-9.

To find the value of K at the intersect of the $\zeta = 0.5$ line and the root loci, we select the Find K option.

```
Option? >f <CR>
```

The program responds:

```
Pick point where |K| is desired
using the mouse and mouse button.
Press any key to continue . . .
```

Click the mouse button after the mouse cursor is pointed at the desired point on the root loci. It may be difficult to pinpoint the exact point on the root loci. However, because for $\zeta = 0.5$, the ratio of the imaginary part to the real part of the root must equal tan(60°), an accurate result may be obtained by adjusting the mouse cursor repeatedly. The following results are obtained at the intersect between the $\zeta = 0.5$ line and the root loci.

Sec. 8.6   Root-Locus Diagram   **97**

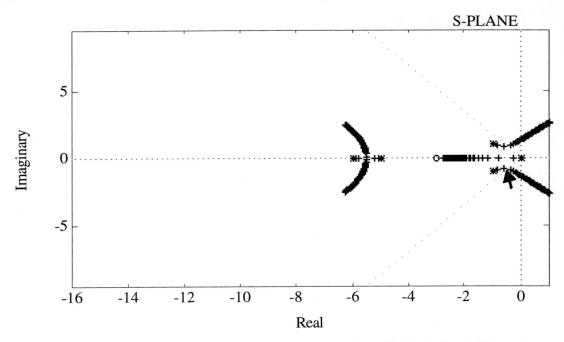

Figure 8-9. Root-locus diagram of Equation 8-37 for $K = 0$ to $K = 400$ with the $\zeta = 0.5$ line and the mouse cursor pointing to the intersect between the root locus and the constant-ζ line.

```
At K = 9.647 the system roots are
-5.7311
-5.3111
-0.4963 + 0.8595i
-0.4963 - 0.8595i
-0.9651
```

The complex roots correspond to a damping ratio very close to the desired value of 0.5.

In a similar manner, the value of K and the corresponding roots at where the root loci cross the $j\omega$-axis can be determined. Selecting the `Marginal K` option, the computer returns

```
Find a jw-axis crossing? (y/n) [n] > y
Enter a value of K that gives Stability [0.001] > <CR>
Enter a value of K that gives INstability [1000] > <CR>
One moment please . . .
A jw-axis crossing occurs at K = 35.52
Associated System Poles are
-5.5804 + 0.7077i
-5.5804 - 0.7077i
-1.8393
```

```
0.0000 + 1.3531i
0.0000 - 1.3531i
Label K on graph? [y/n] [n] >
```

More illustrative examples on the applications of `rlplot` for system design will be given in Chapter 10, Design of Control Systems.

EXERCISES

8-1. Use the CSAD function `routh` to determine the stability of the closed-loop control systems that have the following characteristic equations. Determine the number of roots of each equation that are in the right-half s-plane or on the $j\omega$-axis. Check the answers by solving the equations using the `roots` in the MATLAB toolbox.
(a) $s^3 + 20s^2 + 10s + 100 = 0$
(b) $s^6 + 2s^5 + 8s^4 + 15s^3 + 20s^2 + 16s + 16 = 0$
(c) $s^4 + 2s^3 + 10s^2 + 20s + 5 = 0$
(d) $s^5 + 4s^4 + 8s^3 + 8s^2 + 7s + 4 = 0$

8-2. The open-loop transfer functions of single-loop control systems with unity feedback, $H(s) = 1$, are given subsequently. Find the error constants, K_p, K_v, and K_a, and the steady-state errors to unit-step, unit-ramp, and parabola function $t^2u(t)/2$, inputs, for the stable systems. Use `tfess` in the *CSAD Toolbox*.
(a)

$$G(s) = \frac{100}{s^2 + 12s + 125}$$

(b)

$$G(s) = \frac{100(s + 5)}{s(s + 15)(s + 150)}$$

(c)

$$G(s) = \frac{100}{s^2(s^2 + 10s + 100)}$$

(d)

$$G(s) = \frac{5(s + 1)(s + 5)}{s^2(s^2 + 3s + 1)}$$

8-3. The block diagram of a linear control system is shown in Figure 8P-3, where $r(t)$ is the reference input, and $n(t)$ is the disturbance.

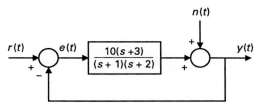

Figure 8P-3.

(a) Find the steady-state error of the system when $n(t) = 0$ and $r(t)$ is the unit-ramp function. Show that the system is stable, and find the roots of the characteristic equation. Use the function ess.

(b) Find the steady-state value of $y(t)$ when $r(t) = 0$ and $n(t)$ is a unit-step function. *Hint:* Use tfcloop to find the closed-loop transfer function with $n(t)$ as input and $y(t)$ as output. Use the MATLAB function polyval to find the final value of $y(t)$ using the final-value theorem.

8-4. The open-loop transfer function of a unity-feedback control system is

$$G(s) = \frac{1}{s(s + 1)^2(1 + T_p)}$$

Compute and plot the unit-step responses of the closed-loop system for $T_p = 0$, 0.5, and 0.707. Use tftplot and enter the denominator polynomial with padd and pmult operating on the numerator and denominator of $G(s)$. Show that the system is marginally stable for $T_p = 0.707$.

8-5. The open-loop transfer function of a unity-feedback control system is

$$G(s) = \frac{1 + T_z s}{s(s + 1)^2}$$

Compute and plot the unit-step responses of the closed-loop system for $T_z = 0$, 0.5, 1.0, 10, and 50. Use the function tftplot, and enter the denominator polynomial with padd and pmult operating on the numerator and denominator of $G(s)$. Comment on the effects of the various values of T_z on the step response.

8-6. Find the closed-loop transfer function of a second-order prototype system that has a damping ratio ζ of 0.707 and a natural undamped frequency ω_n of 20 rd/s. (Use tford2 from the *CSAD Toolbox.*)

8-7. Find the closed-loop transfer function of a second-order prototype system that has a maximum overshoot of 5% and t_{max} of 1.5 s. (The maximum overshoot and t_{max} of the second-order prototype system are given in Equations 8-29 and 8-30, respectively. Use tford2 from the *CSAD Toolbox.*)

8-8. The delay time t_d of the prototype second-order system can be approximated as

$$t_d = \frac{1 + 0.7\zeta}{\omega_n} \qquad 0 < \zeta < 1$$

Consider that the input-output transfer function of a closed-loop control system is

$$\frac{Y(s)}{R(s)} = \frac{100}{s^2 + 5s + 100}$$

Compute the unit-step response of the system. Obtain the attributes of the response and compare the values of t_d, t_r, and t_s computed with those determined using the approximating equation for t_d given previously, and Equations 8-31 and 8-32.

8-9. The closed-loop transfer function of a unity-feedback control system is given as

$$\frac{Y(s)}{R(s)} = \frac{1.5 \times 10^7 K}{s^3 + 3408s^2 + 1{,}204{,}000s + 1.5 \times 10^7 K}$$

For $K = 7$, 14.5, 181.2, and 273.57,

(a) Find the roots of the characteristic equation.

(b) Compute and plot the unit-step response, and find all the attributes.

8-10. The open-loop transfer function of a unity-feedback control system follows:

(a)

$$G(s) = \frac{K(s + 4)}{s(s^2 + 4s + 4)(s + 5)(s + 6)}$$

(b)

$$G(s) = \frac{K}{s(s + 2)(s + 5)(s + 10)}$$

(c)

$$G(s) = \frac{K(s + 3)}{s(s^2 + s + 2)}$$

Compute and plot the root loci for $K \geq 0$. Find the value of K when the system becomes marginally stable. Find the value of K when the relative damping ratio of the roots that are nearest to the $j\omega$-axis is 0.707. Obtain all the properties such as asymptotes, breakaway points, and so on of the root loci.

Frequency-Domain Analysis

9.1. INTRODUCTION

In practice the performance of a control system is more directly measured by its time-domain characteristics. The reason is that the performance of most control systems is best judged based on the time responses resulting from certain test signals. By using computer tools, such as MATLAB and the *CSAD Toolbox*, it is fairly easy to obtain the time responses of control systems and their important attributes such as the maximum overshoot, rise time, delay time, and settling time. However, in the design problem, the difficulties lie in the fact that there are no unified methods of arriving at a designed system given the time-domain performance specifications.

In the frequency-domain the availability of a wealth of graphical methods provide the designer with more convenient design tools for meeting performance specifications.

The transfer function of a closed-loop system with open-loop transfer function $G(s)$ and feedback transfer function $H(s)$ is written

$$M(s) = \frac{Y(s)}{R(s)} = \frac{G(s)}{1 + G(s)H(s)} \tag{9-1}$$

For sinusoidal steady state, we set $s = j\omega$; the last equation becomes

$$M(j\omega) = \frac{Y(j\omega)}{R(j\omega)} = \frac{G(j\omega)}{1 + G(j\omega)H(j\omega)} \qquad (9\text{-}2)$$

Expressing $M(j\omega)$ in terms of its magnitude and phase, we have

$$M(j\omega) = |M(j\omega)| \angle M(j\omega) \qquad (9\text{-}3)$$

where $|M(j\omega)|$ denotes the magnitude and $\angle M(j\omega)$ denotes the phase of $M(j\omega)$, respectively.

Just as with the root-locus technique, most of the analysis and design techniques in the frequency domain rely on the use of the open-loop transfer function to predict the performance of the closed-loop system. The major functions in the *CSAD Toolbox* that are dedicated to analysis and design of linear SISO control systems in the frequency domain are

bplot   Compute and plot Bode plot of the loop transfer function $G(s)H(s)$ so that the stability and the relative stability of the closed-loop system of Equation 9-1 can be determined.

mvpplot   Compute and plot magnitude versus phase of the loop transfer function $G(s)H(s)$ so that the stability and relative stability of the closed-loop system of Equation 9-1 can be determined. Nichols loci can be superposed on the plot to give magnitude information on $M(j\omega)$ when $H(s) = 1$.

plrplot   Compute and plot polar plot for $\omega \geq 0$ of $G(j\omega)H(j\omega)$ for stability studies using the Nyquist criterion.

fddesign   Frequency-domain design of closed-loop systems with a first-order lead or lag controller. Linked to bplot, and tftplot, so this function can be used for analysis purposes.

9.2 FREQUENCY-DOMAIN SPECIFICATIONS

The following performance specifications and measures are often used for the characterization of linear time-invariant systems in the frequency domain.

Peak Resonance M_p: The peak resonance M_p is defined as the maximum value of $|M(j\omega)|$. In general, the magnitude of M_p gives an indication of the relative stability of the closed-loop system. Normally, a large M_p corresponds to a large maximum overshoot of the step response in the time domain. A system with a value of M_p less than or equal to one may indicate that the time response of the system is too slow. When the system's transfer function has poles on the $j\omega$ axis, M_p is infinite. *When the system is unstable*, M_p *ceases to have any meaning.* Generally, it is recommended that the desirable range of M_p should be between 1.1 and 1.5.

For a second-order system that has the prototpye closed-loop transfer function as in Eq. (8-24), M_p is given as

$$M_p = \frac{1}{2\zeta\sqrt{1 - \zeta^2}} \qquad 0 < \zeta \leq 0.707 \qquad (9-4)$$

$M_p = 1$ for $\zeta \geq 0.707$.

Resonant Frequency ω_p: The resonant frequency ω_p is the frequency at which M_p occurs. For the prototype second-order system, ω_p is given as

$$\omega_p = \omega_n\sqrt{1 - 2\zeta^2} \qquad (9-5)$$

Bandwidth: The bandwidth, BW, is the frequency at which the magnitude of $|M(j\omega)|$ drops to 70.7% or 3 dB down from the zero-frequency value. In general, the bandwidth of a control system gives measure of the transient response performances. A large bandwidth corresponds to a faster rise time, because higher-frequency signals are more easily passed on to the output. Conversely, if the bandwidth is small, only signals of relatively low frequencies are passed, and the time response will generally be slow and sluggish. Bandwidth also indicates the noise-filtering characteristics and the robustness of the system.

For the prototype second-order system, bandwidth is given as

$$BW = \omega_n[(1 - 2\zeta^2) + \sqrt{4\zeta^4 - 4\zeta^2 + 2)}]^{1/2} \qquad (9-6)$$

The preceding three performance indices are all measured directly from the closed-loop frequency response plot of $M(j\omega)$. Figure 9-1 illustrates a typical $M(j\omega)$-versus-ω curve with M_p, ω_p and BW indicated.

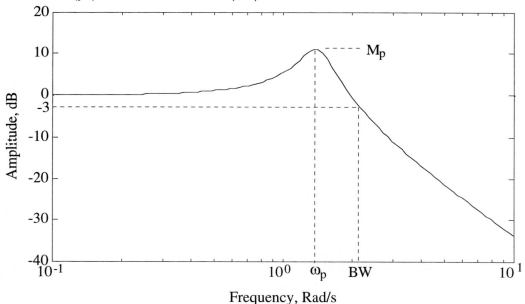

Figure 9-1.   Typical $|M(j\omega)|$ plot of a closed-loop control system.

There are performance indices of the closed-loop system that are measured from the open-loop transfer function $G(j\omega)$ or $G(j\omega)H(j\omega)$. These are the *gain margin* (GM), *gain crossover frequency* (ω_g), *phase margin* (ΦM), and the *phase crossover frequency* (ω_c).

Phase-Crossover Frequency (ω_c):   Phase-crossover frequency is the frequency at which the phase of $G(j\omega)H(j\omega)$ is $-180°$.

Gain-Crossover Frequency (ω_g):   Gain-crossover frequency is the frequency at which the magnitude of $G(j\omega)H(j\omega)$ is unity (or 0 dB).

Gain Margin (GM):   Gain margin is the amount of gain in dB that can be increased in the system loop before the closed-loop system reaches instability. Analytically, GM is given by

$$GM = 20\log_{10} \frac{1}{|G(j\omega_c)H(j\omega_c)|} \text{ dB} \tag{9-7}$$

where ω_c is the phase-crossover frequency in rd/s.

Phase Margin (ΦM):   Phase margin is the amount of phase in degrees that $\angle G(j\omega)H(j\omega)$ can be added at the gain-crossover frequency ω_g before the closed-loop system reaches instability. Analytically, phase margin of $G(s)H(s)$ with poles and zeros all in the left-half s-plane can be expressed as

$$\Phi M = \angle G(j\omega_g)H(j\omega_g) + 180° \tag{9-8}$$

where ω_g is the gain-crossover frequency, and $\angle G(j\omega_g)H(j\omega_g)$ is a negative quantity.

The definitions of the gain and phase margins are shown in the polar plot in Figure 9-2, the Bode plot in Figure 9-3, and the magnitude-phase plot in Figure 9-4, all for the loop-transfer function $G(j\omega)H(j\omega)$.

For the prototype second-order system, the relationship between phase margin and ζ is given as

$$\Phi M \cong \tan^{-1}\left(\frac{2\zeta}{(\sqrt{1 + 4\zeta^4} - 2\zeta^2)^{1/2}}\right) \tag{9-9}$$

Equations 9-4, 9-6, and 9-9 are useful for design purposes. Given the time-domain specifications on maximum overshoot, rise time, and settling time, the corresponding values of M_p, BW, and phase margin in the frequency domain are indicated by these relationships. It should be kept in mind that these equations may not yield accurate results for high-order systems, depending on whether a pair of dominant poles truly exists or not.

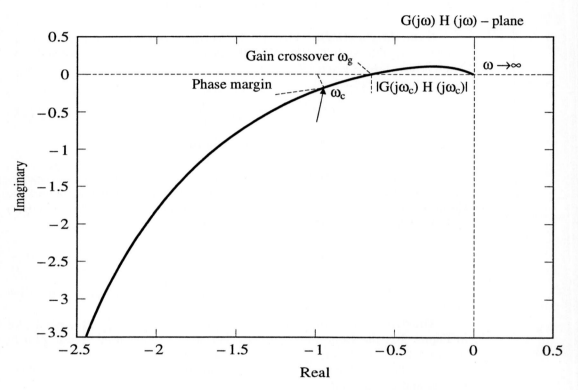

Figure 9-2. Gain and phase margins defined in the polar plot of $G(j\omega)H(j\omega)$-plane.

Chap. 9   **Frequency-Domain Analysis**

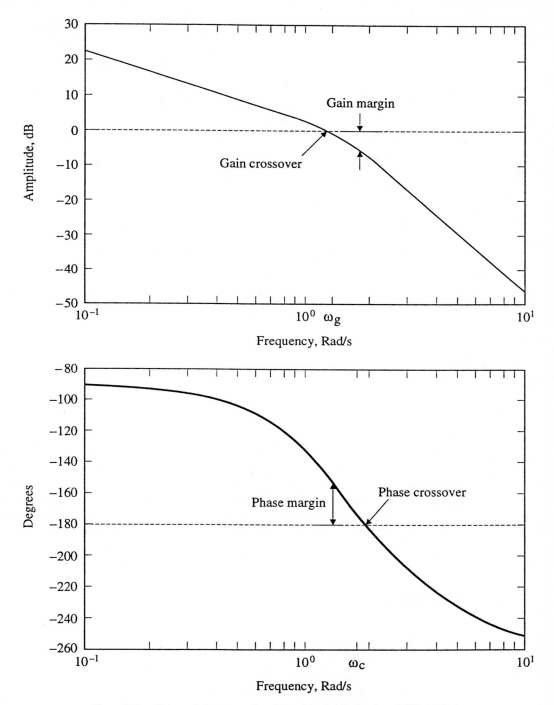

Figure 9-3. Gain and phase margins defined in the Bode plot of $G(j\omega)H(j\omega)$.

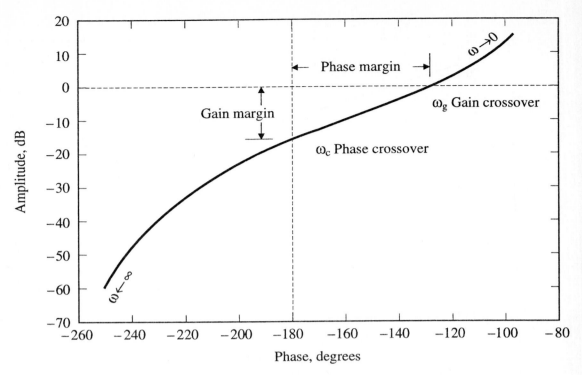

Figure 9-4. Gain and phase margins defined in the magnitude-versus-phase plot of $G(j\omega)H(j\omega)$.

9.3 STABILITY ANALYSIS IN THE FREQUENCY DOMAIN

Stability analysis of a linear closed-loop SISO system with loop transfer function $G(s)H(s)$ can be conducted by use of the polar plot, the Bode plot, or the magnitude-phase plot of $G(j\omega)H(j\omega)$. The two latter types of plots, strictly, are useful for minimum-phase transfer functions, that is, ones that do not have poles or zeros in the right-half s-plane. Details on the stability of linear control systems in the frequency domain can be found in standard texts on control theory and are not elaborated on here. The material presented in the following is designed only for the applications of the functions in the *CSAD Toolbox*.

9.3.1 The Nyquist Criterion (Minimum-Phase Systems)

Given the loop transfer function $G(s)H(s)$ of a minimum-phase transfer function of a single-loop control system whose closed-loop transfer function is given in Equation 9-1, the Nyquist plot is the plot of $G(j\omega)H(j\omega)$ for $\omega = 0$ to $\omega = \infty$. The closed-loop system is stable if the critical point $(-1, j0)$ of the $G(j\omega)H(j\omega)$-plane is not enclosed by the Nyquist plot. The $(-1, j0)$ point is said to be

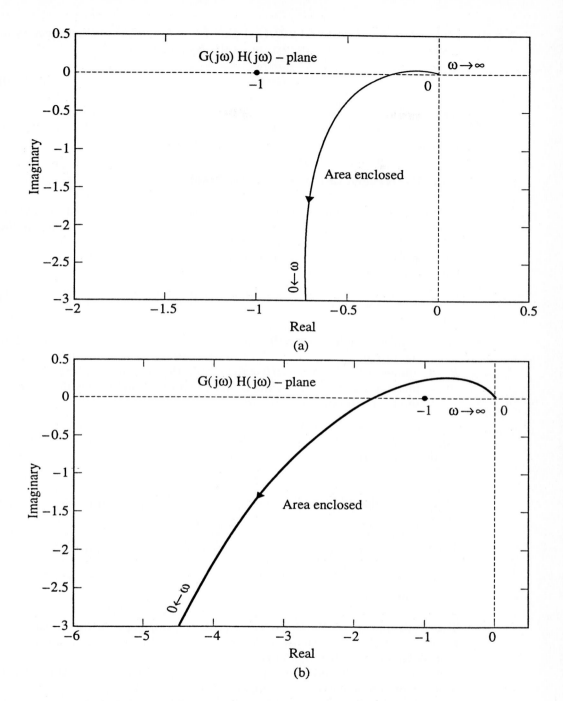

Figure 9-5. (a) The critical point $(-1, j0)$ is not enclosed. The closed-loop system is stable. (b) The critical point $(-1, j0)$ is enclosed. The closed-loop system is unstable.

enclosed by the Nyquist $G(j\omega)H(j\omega)$ plot if it is to the left of the trajectory as ω varies from ∞ to 0. Figure 9-5 shows the Nyquist plots of

$$G(s)H(s) = \frac{K}{s(s + 1)(s + 2)} \qquad (9\text{-}10)$$

for two values of K. In Figure 9-5(a), $K = 1$, the $(-1, j0)$ point is not enclosed, and the closed-loop system is stable. In Figure 9-5(b), $K = 10$, the critical point is enclosed, and the closed-loop system is unstable.

9.3.2 The Nyquist Criterion (General Case)

A more general Nyquist criterion that can be applied to minimum as well as nonminimum-phase transfer functions is described below. Briefly, given the Nyquist plot of $G(j\omega)H(j\omega)$, such as those shown in Figure 9-5, the Nyquist criterion for stability of the closed-loop system is that the following equation must be satisfied:

$$\Phi_{11} = -(0.5P_\omega + P_{-1})180° \qquad (9\text{-}11)$$

where

$P_\omega =$ number of poles of $G(s)H(s)$ that are on the $j\omega$-axis in the s-plane including the origin

$P_{-1} =$ number of poles of $G(s)H(s)$ that are in the right-half s-plane

$\Phi_{11} =$ phase angle traversed by the Nyquist plot of $G(j\omega)H(j\omega)$ with respect to the $(-1, j0)$ point as ω is varied from ∞ to 0

For the transfer function of Equation 9-10, $P_\omega = 1$ (one pole on the $j\omega$-axis), and $P_{-1} = 0$. Equation 9-11 gives the value of Φ_{11} that must be satisfied for the system to be stable.

$$\Phi_{11} = -90° \qquad (9\text{-}12)$$

which means that the phasor drawn from the $\omega = \infty$ point to the $\omega = 0$ point on the Nyquist plot must traverse a net angle of $-90°$, where the minus sign means clockwise direction. Figure 9-6(a) shows that when $K = 1$, $\Phi_{11} = -90°$, which satisfies Equation 9-12, and the system is stable. In Figure 9-6(b), $\Phi_{11} = +270°$, and the system is unstable.

9.3.3 The Bode Plot

The Bode plot of $G(j\omega)H(j\omega)$ consists of $|G(j\omega)H(j\omega)|$ in dB versus ω in rad/second and $\angle G(j\omega)H(j\omega)$ in degrees versus ω. Figure 9-7 shows the Bode plots of the transfer function in Equation 9-10 with $K = 1$ and $K = 10$. Notice that when K is increased from 1 to 10, the magnitude curve is raised by 20 dB, whereas the phase curve is unchanged.

The stability of the closed-loop system can be investigated from the Bode plot by observing the magnitude of $G(j\omega)H(j\omega)$ at the phase crossover, and the

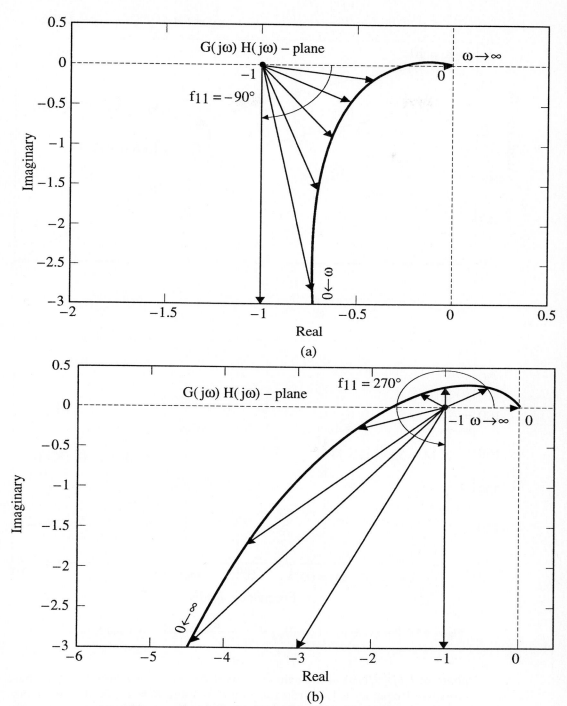

Figure 9-6. (a) Stable closed-loop system. (b) Unstable closed-loop system.

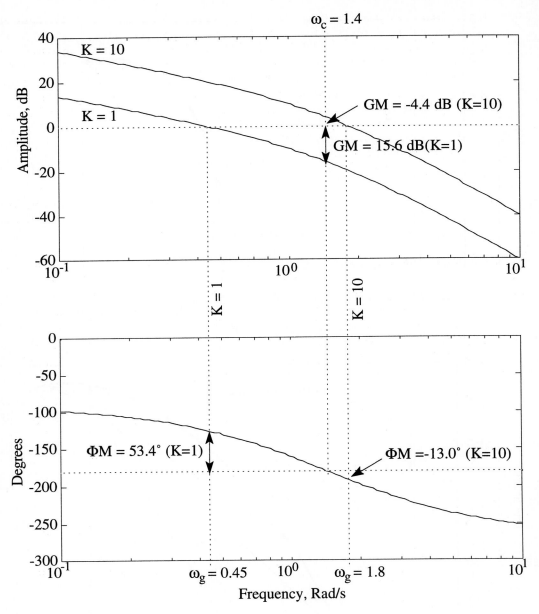

Figure 9-7. Bode diagrams of $G(s)H(s) = \dfrac{K}{s(s + 1)(s + 2)}$ for $K = 1$ and $K = 10$.

phase of $G(j\omega)H(j\omega)$ at the gain crossover. As shown in Figure 9-7, the phase crossover frequency is 1.414 rd/s for both $K = 1$ and $K = 10$. At this frequency, the magnitude of $G(j\omega)H(j\omega)$ is -15.56 dB for $K = 1$. This corresponds to the

Nyquist plot of $G(j\omega)H(j\omega)$ intersecting the negative real axis to the right of the $(-1, j0)$ point, and the system is stable. The gain margin for $K = 1$ is 15.56 dB. When $K = 10$, the magnitude of $G(j\omega)H(j\omega)$ at $\omega_c = 1.414$ rad/s is 4.437 dB. This corresponds to the Nyquist plot intersecting the negative axis to the left of the $(-1, j0)$ point, and the system is unstable. The gain margin of the unstable system is -4.437 dB.

When $K = 1$ the gain-crossover frequency is 0.4458 rad/s. At this frequency the phase of $G(j\omega)H(j\omega)$ is $-126.59°$. Thus, the phase margin is determined from Equation 9-8.

$$\Phi M = -126.59 + 180 = 53.41° \qquad (9\text{-}13)$$

and the system is stable.

When $K = 10$, the gain-crossover frequency is 1.802 rad/s. At this frequency the phase of $G(j\omega)H(j\omega)$ is $-192.99°$, which corresponds to a phase margin of $-12.99°$, and the system is unstable.

9.3.4 The Magnitude-versus-Phase Plot

The magnitude-versus-phase plot of $G(j\omega)H(j\omega)$ is the plot of the magnitude of $G(j\omega)H(j\omega)$ in dB versus the phase of $G(j\omega)H(j\omega)$. Figure 9-8 shows the magnitude-versus-phase plot of the transfer function in Equation 9-10 for $K = 1$ and $K = 10$. The gain and phase crossover points are located as shown in Figure 9-8. From these crossover points, the gain and phase margins of the system with $K = 1$ and $K = 10$ are shown.

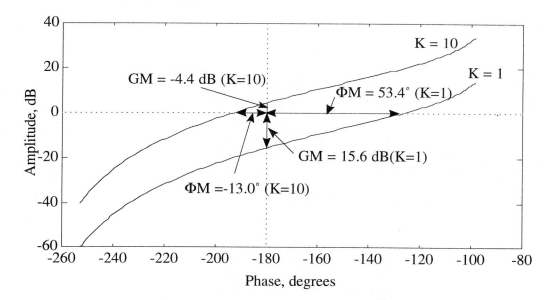

Figure 9-8. Magnitude-versus-phase plot of $G(s)H(s) = \dfrac{K}{s(s+1)(s+2)}$ for $K = 1$ and $K = 10$.

9.4 CSAD FUNCTIONS FOR FREQUENCY-DOMAIN ANALYSIS

9.4.1 bplot

The function bplot in the *CSAD Toolbox* is an interactive program for computing and plotting Bode plots of transfer functions with or without a pure time delay.

Let us illustrate the application of bplot with the following loop transfer function.

$$G(s)H(s) = \frac{5(s + 1)}{s(s + 2)(s^2 + 2s + 2)} \qquad (9\text{-}14)$$

One way of executing bplot is to enter bplot <CR> at the MATLAB prompt.

```
>>bplot <CR>
Default input is: 2
Enter Numerator Polynomial>[5 5]
Default input is: s^2 + 2s^1 + 2
Enter Denominator Polynomial>pmult([1 0],[1 2],[1 2 2])
Enter START frequency w=10^k1, k1 = [-1]> <CR> (Choose 0.1 rad/s)
Enter END frequency w=10^k2, k2 = [1]> <CR> (Choose 10 rad/s)
```

```
                         -BODEPLOT OPTIONS-

                   Amplitude      Freq range
                   Phase          Time delay
                   Both           New TF
                   Zoom in        Display TF
                   Set axes       Margins
                   Grid           Roots
                   Hold           View Data
                   Label          Quit
        Option?>a <CR>      (Select Amplitude option)
```

The magnitude plot of $G(j\omega)H(j\omega)$ is plotted as shown in Figure 9-9. By selecting the phase option the phase of $G(j\omega)H(j\omega)$ is plotted as shown as the bottom part of Figure 9-9. The magnitude and phase plots can also be obtained simultaneously by choosing both. By selecting Margins, the performance data are calculated and displayed.

```
Gain margin, dB          5.054
Phase crossover, rad/s   1.799
Phase margin, degrees    25.7
Gain crossover, rad/s    1.309
Peak Resonance, dB       8.463
Peak Resonance, |Mp|     2.649
3 dB bandwidth, rad/s    2.048
```

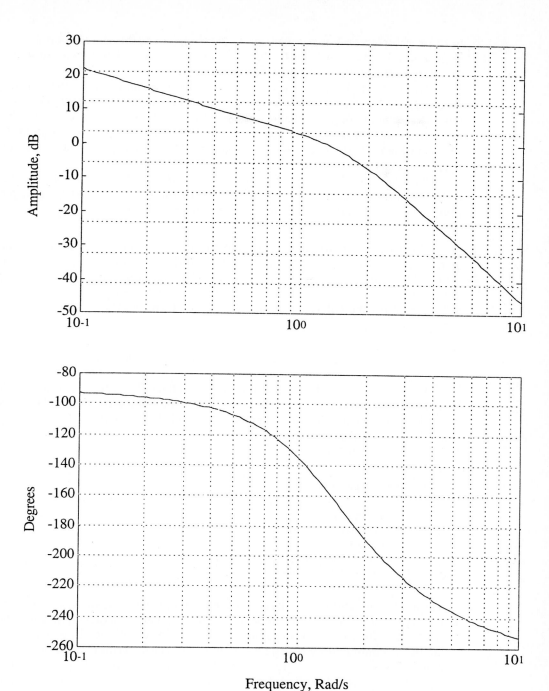

Figure 9-9. Bode plot of $G(s)H(s) = \dfrac{5(s+1)}{s(s+2)(s^2+2s+2)}$.

Sec. 9.4   CSAD Functions for Frequency-Domain Analysis   **115**

Because the gain and phase margins are both positive, the closed-loop system represented by the loop transfer function in Equation 9-14 is stable, although the margin of stability is not great.

To get the Bode plot of the closed-loop system, we may reenter the transfer function data by selecting New T''. The numerator polynomial is still $5(s + 1)$, but the denominator polynomial is $s(s + 2)(s^2 + 2s + 2) + 5(s + 1)$. The magnitude and phase plots of the closed-loop transfer function are plotted as shown in Figure 9-10. The maximum value of $|M(j\omega)|$ agrees with the value of peak resonance given above.

With the closed-loop transfer function entered, do not select the Margins *option, as the results will represent another closed-loop system with the transfer function you just entered as the open-loop transfer function.*

As a next step we can investigate the effect of pure time delay on the performance of the system. Notice that this is difficult to do in the time domain, and we have to approximate the time delay by a rational function using the function tddelay. Selecting the Time delay option of bplot, the function will prompt for the value of the time delay, to which we arbitrarily enter 0.5 s.

```
Option?>t <CR>
Enter desired time delay in seconds [0]>0.5 <CR>
```

Figure 9-11 shows the phase plot of $G(j\omega)H(j\omega)e^{0.5j\omega}$, along with that with zero time delay, from $\omega = 0.1$ to 10 rad/s. Because the pure time delay does not affect the magnitude, the magnitude plot on the top part of Figure 9-9 is not affected. Selecting Margins, the performance data when the time delay is 0.5 s is displayed below.

Gain margin, dB	−1.295
Phase crossover, rad/s	1.178
Phase margin, degrees	−11.78
Gain crossover: rad/s	1.309
Peak Resonance, dB	inf
Peak Resonance: $|M_p|$	inf
3dB bandwidth, rad/s	1.801

Because the gain and phase margins are negative, when time delay is 0.5 s, the system is unstable. The result on peak resonance given is incorrect, because the correct value for M_p for an unstable system should be infinite. In general, the value of M_p computed by Margins may be subject to scrutiny even for stable systems. For systems with large M_p the limited number of data points in the computation of the closed-loop frequency response may cause the computation of the peak value of $|M(j\omega)|$ to be inaccurate. For an unstable system the result on bandwidth will also be meaningless.

The effect of pure time delay in the open-loop transfer function on closed-

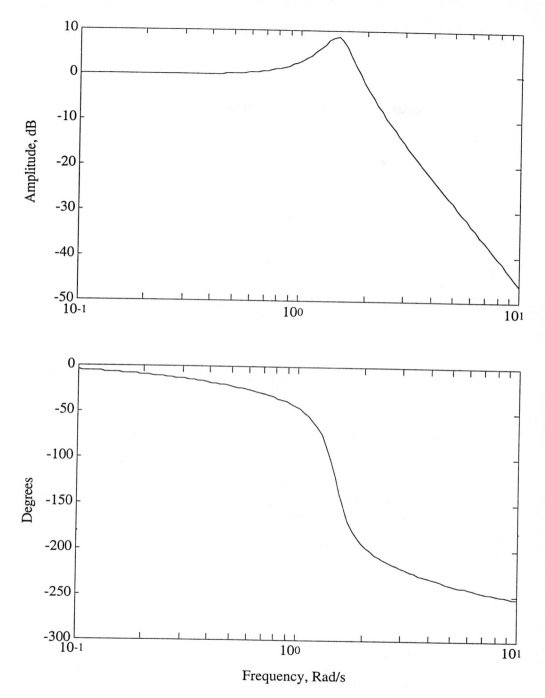

Figure 9-10. Closed-loop frequency response of the system with $G(s)H(s) = \dfrac{5(s + 1)}{s(s + 2)(s^2 + 2s + 2)}$.

Sec. 9.4   CSAD Functions for Frequency-Domain Analysis   **117**

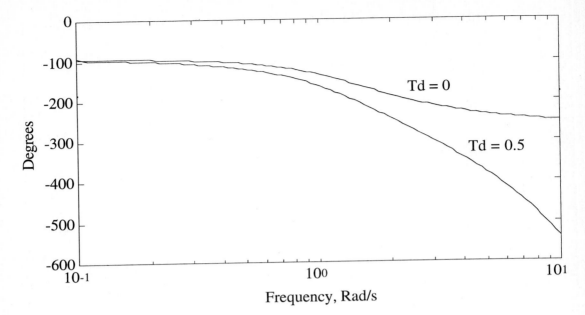

Figure 9-11. Phase plot of $G(s)H(s) = \dfrac{5(s + 1)e^{-T_d s}}{s(s + 2)(s^2 + 2s + 2)}$.

loop system is clearly shown by the phase plot in Figure 9-11. Because the phase of the open-loop system is reduced by the amount of $-\omega T_d$, where T_d is the time delay in seconds, while the magnitude curve is not affected, the phase crossover frequency is reduced (from 1.799 to 1.178 rad/s), and the phase and gain margins are reduced.

Let us find the critical value of T_d so that the closed-loop system is marginally stable. This may be done by trial and error using the options Time delay and Margins repeatedly. The objective is to find the value of T_d so that the gain and phase margins are zero. After a few trial-and-error runs, the following results are obtained when $T_d = 0.3429$ s.

```
Gain margin, dB              -0.0006499
Phase crossover, rad/s        1.308
Phase margin, degrees        -0.005133
Gain crossover, rad/s         1.309
Peak Resonance, dB            inf
Peak Resonance, |Mp|          inf
3dB bandwidth, rad/s          1.896
```

9.4.2 plrplot

The function plrplot of the *CSAD Toolbox* computes the frequency response of $G(j\omega)H(j\omega)$ and plots the data in the polar coordinates. Figure 9-2 is an example of a polar plot done by plrplot.

9.4.3 mvpplot

The function `mvpplot` of the *CSAD Toolbox* computes the frequency response of $G(j\omega)H(j\omega)$ and plots the data in the magnitude-versus-phase coordinates. The magnitude-versus-phase plot provides information on the magnitude of the closed-loop system with unity feedback $[H(s) = 1]$ via the Nichols chart. The Nichols loci are a set of trajectories on which the value of $|M(j\omega)|$ (or simply M) is constant. Selecting `Nichols` from the `mvpplot` options, the following message will be given:

```
Nichols magnitude curves for 9, 6, 3, 1, 0, -1, -3, -6, -9 dB.
The -3-dB curve is dot-dashed; the others are dotted.
Press any key to continue . . .
```

Figure 9-12 shows the magnitude-versus-phase plot of the transfer function in Equation 9-14 with the Nichols loci superimposed. It is assumed in this case that $G(s)$ is the entire open-loop transfer function, and $H(s) = 1$. In other words, the Nichols chart is valid only for systems with unity feedback. The largest value of M corresponds to the closed trajectory that is closest to the 0-dB/$-180°$-point. In Figure 9-12 the Nichols locus for $M = 9$ dB is tangent to the $G(j\omega)$ locus, which corresponds to $M_p = 9$ dB. The actual value of M_p calculated by the "Margins" option is 8.463 dB. The frequency on the $G(j\omega)$ curve at the intersect with the $M = -3$-dB locus is the BW of the closed-loop system.

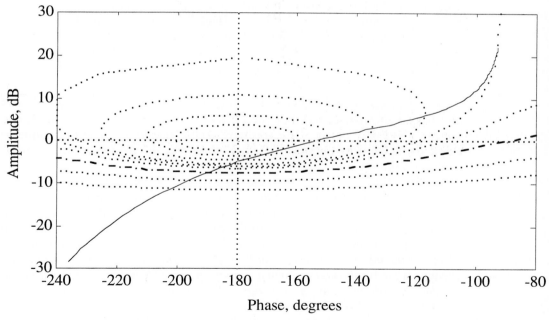

Figure 9-12. Magnitude-versus-phase plot with Nichols chart for $G(s) = \dfrac{5(s+1)}{s(s+2)(s^2+2s+2)}$.

9.4.4 Using the `fddesign` Program for Frequency-Domain Analysis

The frequency-domain design function `fddesign` in the *CSAD Toolbox* has several useful features that make it attractive for analysis purposes. The options menu of `fddesign` is

```
- FDDESIGN OPTIONS -
Controller values
Frequency Response
Lead/Lag math
Goals to meet
Steady-state Error
Step Response
Display TF's
Poles and Zeros
New Plant TF
Quit
```

The transfer function of the controller in `fddesign` is

$$G_c(s) = \frac{K(1 + aTs)}{(1 + Ts)} \tag{9-15}$$

where a and T are real constants. Using `fddesign` for analysis purposes, enter $K = 1$, $a = 1$ and $T = 1$; *not* $K = 1$, $a = 0$ and $T = 0$. Selecting the `Frequency Response` option, the following selection will appear:

```
Response of K*plant, Lead/Lag, Open-loop, Closed-loop? [O]>
```

Choosing `Open-loop` will give the Bode plot of the open-loop transfer function. As an alternative, you may choose $K = 1$ and any values for a and T, and use the `K*plant` option. The `Closed-loop` option is a feature unique to `fddesign`, which computes the closed-loop frequency response from information on the open-loop transfer function.

When the `Frequency response` option is selected, `fddesign` will link to `bplot` automatically. After the frequency response is completed, entering `Quit <CR>` from `bplot` will return to `fddesign`. As an illustration, the amplitude frequency response of the closed-loop system described by Equation 9-14 is computed using `fddesign`, and the same plots shown in Figure 9-10 are obtained. *Do not select the `Margins` option after the closed-loop frequency, as the result will represent a system with the closed-loop transfer function as the open-loop transfer function.* To obtain the information in M_p and BW of the closed-loop system, you should return to the options menu of `fddesign` and select `Frequency Response`, choose the open-loop frequency response, and then follow by `Margins`.

EXERCISES

9-1. The open-loop transfer functions of unity-feedback control systems are given in the following. Compute and plot the Bode plots of $G(j\omega)$ and of the closed-loop transfer function. Use the function `fddesign` from the *CSAD Toolbox*. Find the gain margin, phase margin, M_p and BW of the closed-loop system.

(a)

$$G(s) = \frac{5}{s(1 + 0.5s)(1 + 0.1s)}$$

(b)

$$G(s) = \frac{20}{s(1 + 0.5s)(1 + 0.1s)}$$

(c)

$$G(s) = \frac{500}{(s + 1.5)(s + 5)(s + 10)}$$

(d)

$$G(s) = \frac{1}{2s(s^2 + s + 1)}$$

(e)

$$G(s) = \frac{100e^{-s}}{s(s^2 + 10s + 100)}$$

9-2. The open-loop transfer function of a unity-feedback control system is

$$G(s) = \frac{Ts + 1}{2s(s^2 + s + 1)}$$

Compute and plot the Bode plots of $G(j\omega)$ and of the closed-loop transfer function for $T = 0.05, 1, 2, 3, 4$, and 5. Find the gain margin, phase margin, M_p and BW of the closed-loop system.

9-3. The open-loop transfer function of a unity-feedback control system is

$$G(s) = \frac{1}{2s(s^2 + s + 1)(Ts + 1)}$$

Repeat Problem 9-2 with $T = 0, 0.5, 1, 2, 3, 4$, and 5.

9-4. The loop transfer function $G(s)H(s)$ of single-loop feedback control systems are given subsequently. Compute and plot the polar plot of $G(j\omega)H(j\omega)$ for $\omega = 0$ to $\omega = \infty$. Determine the stability of the closed-loop system using the Nyquist criterion. If the system transfer function is of the nonminimum-phase type, use the Nyquist criterion given by Equation 9-7.

(a)

$$G(s)H(s) = \frac{20}{s(1 + 0.1s)(1 + 0.5s)}$$

(b)

$$G(s)H(s) = \frac{10}{s(1 + 0.1s)(1 + 0.5s)}$$

(c)

$$G(s)H(s) = \frac{0.1}{s(s + 1)(s^2 + s + 1)}$$

(d)

$$G(s)H(s) = \frac{10}{s^2(1 + 0.2s)(1 + 0.5s)}$$

(e)

$$G(s)H(s) = \frac{3(s + 2)}{s(s^3 + 3s + 1)}$$

(f)

$$G(s)H(s) = \frac{s^2 - 5s + 2}{s(s^3 + 2s^2 + 2s + 10)}$$

9-5. The loop-transfer functions $G(s)H(s)$ of single-loop feedback control systems are given subsequently. Compute and plot the polar plots for $K = 1$ $\omega = 0$ to $\omega = \infty$. From the gain margin and the polar plot find the values of K for the system to be stable.

(a)

$$G(s)H(s) = \frac{K}{s(s + 2)(s + 10)}$$

(b)

$$G(s)H(s) = \frac{K(s + 1)}{s(s + 2)(s + 5)(s + 10)}$$

(c)

$$G(s)H(s) = \frac{Ke^{-s}}{s(s + 1)(s + 2)}$$

9-6. The open-loop transfer function of unity-feedback control systems are given subsequently. Compute and plot the magnitude-versus-phase plots for the systems. Find the gain margin, phase margin, and M_p and BW if the system is stable.

(a)

$$G(s) = \frac{10}{s(1 + 0.1s)(1 + 0.5s)}$$

(b)

$$G(s) = \frac{e^{-s}}{s(0.01s^2 + 0.1s + 1)}$$

10

Design of Control Systems

10.1 INTRODUCTION

Because conventional design of control systems rely to a great extent on the process of trial and error and intuition, many functions in the *CSAD Toolbox* can be used for design purposes. All the functions in the *CSAD Toolbox* under Interactive Plotting and Control System Analysis and Design described in Part 3 can be used for the design of linear SISO control systems.

The time-domain design of control systems refers to the use of the time-domain properties and specifications of the system to be designed. In general, the time-domain design of linear control systems is carried out by working with the poles and zeros of the transfer function in the *s*-plane. The CSAD functions, `iltplot`, `rlplot`, `svplot`, `tftplot`, `svstuff`, and `tddesign` are useful for design in the time-domain.

Design in the frequency domain can be carried out using the Bode plot, polar plot, or the magnitude-versus-phase plot. Thus, the CSAD functions, `bplot`, `mvpplot`, `plrplot`, and the `fddesign`, all can be used for design purposes. The most useful functions for general design purposes are `tddesign` and `fddesign`, although the former is basically intended for PID control, and the latter is dedicated to a first-order lead-lag controller.

Most of the conventional design methods in control systems rely on the so-called fixed-configuration design in that the designer at the outset decides the place where the controller is to be positioned relative to the controlled process or plant. Figure 10-1 illustrates several commonly used system configurations with controllers. The most commonly used system configuration is the *series* or *cascade controller* shown in Figure 10-1(a). In Figure 10-1(b), the system has a feedback controller. Figure 10-1(c) shows a system that generates the control signal by feeding back the state variables through constant real gains, and the scheme is known as *state feedback*. Systems with all these and other controller configurations can be designed with the various CSAD programs by first getting the transfer functions or the dynamic equations in the proper form.

10.2 THE PID CONTROLLER

One of the most popular controllers used in practice for the compensation of control systems is the PID series controller. The letters PID stand for *proportional*, *integral*, and *derivative*. The transfer function of the basic PID controller is

$$G_c(s) = K_p + K_d s + \frac{K_i}{s} \tag{10-1}$$

where K_p, K_d, and K_i are real constants. The design problem involves the determination of the values of these three constants so that the performance of the system meets the design requirements.

The derivative control introduces a signal that is proportional to the derivative of the actuating signal in the system loop, and the general effect is to improve the damping of the closed-loop system. Derivative control does not affect the steady-state of the system output.

The integral control introduces a signal that is proportional to the integral of the actuating signal in the system loop. Integral control improves the steady-state error of the closed-loop system, and by properly designing the integral-control constant K_i, the damping of the transient response can also be improved, although at the expense of rise and settling times.

The design of the PID controller can be carried out by artificially dividing the controller into a PD portion and a PI portion. The method is outlined as follows:

1. Consider that the PID controller consists of a PI portion connected in cascade with a PD portion. The PID-controller transfer function is partitioned as

$$G_c(s) = K_p + K_d s + \frac{K_i}{s} = \left(1 + K_{d1}s\right)\left(K_{p2} + \frac{K_{i2}}{s}\right) \tag{10-2}$$

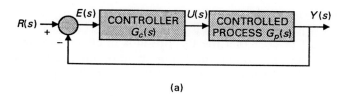

(a)

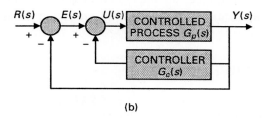

(b)

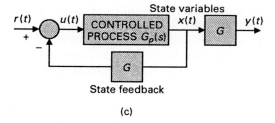

(c)

Figure 10-1. (a) System with series or cascade controller. (b) System with feedback controller. (c) System with state feedback.

The proportional constant of the PD portion is set to unity, because we need only three parameters in the PID controller. Equating both sides of Equation 10-2, we have

$$K_p = K_{p2} + K_{d1}K_{i2} \tag{10-3}$$

$$K_d = K_{d1}K_{p2} \tag{10-4}$$

$$K_i = K_{i2} \tag{10-5}$$

2. Consider that the PI portion is in effect only and select the values of K_{i2} and K_{p2} so that the requirement on the rise time of the system is satisfied. The steady-state error of the system is improved by one order by the PI control. Do not be concerned by the maximum overshoot at this stage, as it may be larger than desired.
3. Use the PD portion to reduce the maximum overshoot. Select the value of K_{d1} to meet the maximum overshoot requirement.
4. The values of K_p, K_d, and K_i are found using Equations 10-3 to 10-5.

10.3 DESIGN WITH tddesign

The function tddesign in the *CSAD Toolbox* is intended as a menu-driven program for the design of a linear control system with a series PID controller. However, the function can be applied to the design of any controller in the time domain simply by setting $K_p = 1$, $K_d = 0$, and $K_i = 0$. The combination of the controller transfer function $G_c(s)$ and process transfer function $G_p(s)$ is entered as the plant transfer function.

As an illustrative example of using tddesign for designing the PID controller in the time domain, let us consider that the controlled process or plant of a control system with unity feedback is described by

$$G_p(s) = \frac{K}{s(s + 5)(s + 10)} \tag{10-6}$$

The performance specifications of the system are given as

Maximum overshoot $\le 4\%$
Steady-state error to unit-ramp ≤ 0.01
Rise time ≤ 0.8 s
Settling time ≤ 0.8 s

To satisfy the steady-state error requirement, K must be ≥ 5000. We can easily show that when $K = 5000$, the closed-loop system is unstable.

10.3.1 The PD-Controller Design

Let us first use a PD controller with $K_i = 0$ in Equation 10-1. The open-loop transfer function of the compensated system with K set at 5000 is

$$G(s) = G_c(s)G_p(s) = \frac{5000K_d(s + K_p/K_d)}{s(s + 5)(s + 10)} \qquad (10\text{-}7)$$

The objective of the design is to maintain the steady-state error because of the unit-ramp input at 0.01, while simultaneously satisfying the transient performance requirement.

The options menu of tddesign is

```
            -TDDESIGN OPTIONS-

            Controller values
            Root locus
            Step Response
            Goals to meet
            Error constants
            Display TF's
            Poles and Zeros
            New Plant RF
            Quit
```

After entering the plant transfer function of Equation 10-6 with $K = 5000$, and $K_p = 1$, $K_d = 0$, $K_i = 0$ for the controller, we select the Goals to meet option. The time-domain specifications are entered at the prompts.

```
Enter Max % Overshoot [0] > 4
Enter Min Rise Time [100] > 0.8
Enter Min Settling Time [100] > 0.8
```

The program returns

```
Estimated Minimum Zeta required is: 0.7156
Estimated Minimum Wn required is: 7.029
```

The minimum value of ζ is determined from the maximum overshoot relationship in Equation 8-29. tddesign substitutes $\zeta = 0.7156$ and $t_r = 0.8$ into Equation 8-31 to find the minimum required value for ω_n, and the result is 2.7444 rad/s. From Equation 8-32 with $t_s = 0.8$, the computed minimum value for ω_n is 7.029 rad/s. Thus, the larger value of ω_n is selected by tddesign. The computed minimum values for ζ and ω_n should be used only as a guideline in the design, because Equations 8-29, 8-31, and 8-32 are valid only for the prototype second-order system. The plant transfer function is of the third order, and with the PID controller, the compensated system will be of the fourth order.

Select the Root locus option next, with $K_p = 1$, $K_i = 0$, and K_d as the variable parameter. Figure 10-2 shows the root locus plot for $0 \leq K_d < \infty$ of the characteristic equation

$$s^3 + 15s^2 + (50 + 5000K_d)s + 5000 = 0 \qquad (10\text{-}8)$$

which is obtained from Equation 10-7. The root loci show the limitation of the PD controller in this case in improving the transient response of the system. Although the two complex roots of the characteristic equation are brought into the left-half plane as K_d increases, the effective amount of damping that can be gained by increasing K_d is limited. As K_d increases, the two complex roots approach 90° and $-90°$, respectively, toward the asymptotes that intersect at -7.5. It is apparent that the minimum damping ratio of 0.7156 cannot even be approached with any value of K_d. In fact, the root locus plot in Figure 10-2 shows that the maximum relative damping ratio that can be realized by the two complex roots is approximately 16%, and the corresponding value of K_d is approximately 0.25. Furthermore, as K_d becomes very large, the real root will be very close to the origin, which may contribute significantly to the maximum overshoot. The conclusion is that although the PD control will stabilize the system, the amount of damping that can be realized is limited.

The transfer function in Equation 10-7 with $K_p = 1$ is entered as the plant transfer function to tddesign. The step response of the closed-loop system

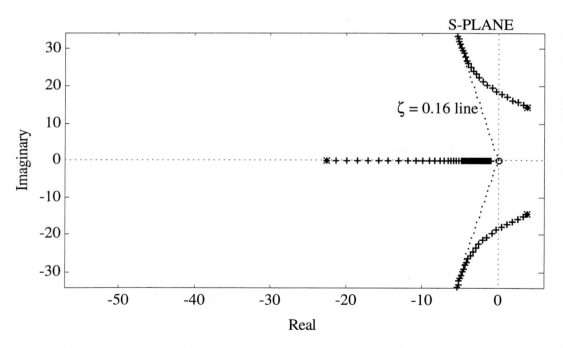

Figure 10-2. Root-locus plot of $s^3 + 15s^2 + (50 + 5000K_d)s + 5000 = 0$ for $0 \leq K_d < \infty$.

when K_d varies is to be determined. For this exercise K_i is set to zero in tdde-sign. When the Step response option is selected from tddesign, the closed-loop function is formed and the function tftplot is called. A word of caution on the process of changing the value of K_d (or any system parameter, in general) is *to make the change in* tddesign, *and not in* tftplot. The reason being that the transfer function that resides in tftplot is the closed-loop transfer function which contains K_d in the numerator as well as the de-nominator. It would be simpler and safer to return to tddesign first by entering Quit from the tftplot menu, choose the "New Plant TF" option in tdde-sign, and then go to Step response or whatever other options.

By varying K_d and obtaining the step response, the following attributes are obtained:

K_d	RISE TIME t_r (s)	SETTLING TIME t_s (s)	% MAX OVERSHOOT
0.10	1.132	0.05	70.2
0.25	0.03305	0.5455	59.4
0.28	0.03107	0.5091	60.7
0.30	0.03012	0.497	60.7
0.50	0.02481	0.4364	64.3
1.0	0.01831	0.400	69.2

Again, in obtaining these attributes you should first observe the quality of the step response and reset the final time if necessary. Otherwise, the attributes computed may be inaccurate.

The preceding tabulation clearly shows that the optimal value of K_d with respect to the maximum overshoot is approximately 0.25. The unit-step response is shown in Figure 10-3.

10.3.2 The PI-Controller Design

Now consider that the process described in Equation 10-6 is compensated by a PI controller of Equation 10-1 with $K_d = 0$. The open-loop transfer function of the compensated system is

$$G(s) = G_c(s)G_p(s) = \frac{5000K_p(s + K_i/K_p)}{s^2(s + 5)(s + 10)} \tag{10-8}$$

Now because the ramp-error constant K_v is infinite, the steady-state error re-sulting from a ramp input is zero, regardless of the value of K, which remains to be 5000.

The "trick" of designing the PI controller is to set the value of K_i/K_p to be significantly smaller than the dominant pole of $G_p(s)$, which in this case is at $s = -5$. Let us set K_i/K_p to be 0.1. The transient behavior of the PI-compensated

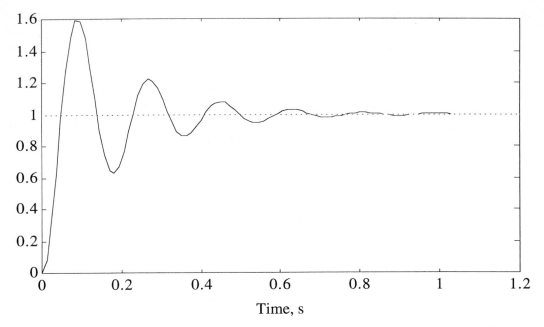

Figure 10-3. Unit-step response of system with open-loop transfer function in Equation 10-7. $K_p = 1$ and $K_d = 0.25$.

system is very similar to that of the original system with the transfer function in Equation 10-6 but with the gain factor replaced by $5000K_p$, that is,

$$G(s) = \frac{5000K_p(s + 0.1)}{s^2(s + 5)(s + 10)} \cong \frac{5000K_p}{s(s + 5)(s + 10)} \qquad (10\text{-}9)$$

It should be emphasized that the approximation in the last equation can only be applied for the transient response and not in the steady state. Now the value of K_p can be selected to give a satisfactory maximum overshoot. Figure 10-4 shows the unit-step responses of the system with the PI controller for $K_p = 0.012$, 0.0163, and 0.02, and $K_i/K_p = 0.1$. The $K_p = 0.163$ case corresponds to a relative damping ratio of 0.707, and the roots of the characteristic equation are at -11.18, $-1.91 \pm j1.91$. The attributes of the unit-step responses are tabulated below for six different values of K_p.

K_p	t_r (SEC)	t_s (SEC)	y_{max} (%)
0.012	1.061	6.869	8.0
0.0163	0.7732	3.232	10.3
0.020	0.637	2.323	13.8
0.024	0.5411	1.919	18.1
0.030	0.4494	1.616	24.5
0.040	0.3697	2.727	34.2

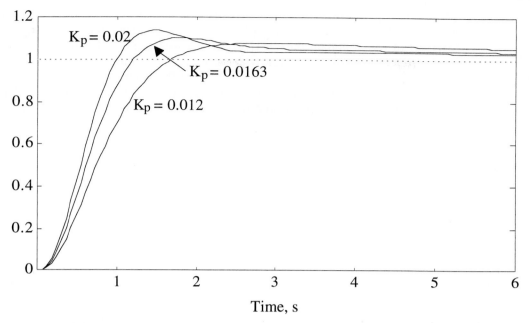

Figure 10-4. Unit-step responses of system with open-loop transfer function in Equation 10-8 with $K_i/K_p = 0.1$; $K_p = 0.012$, 0.0163, and 0.02.

From these results it became apparent that a lower maximum overshoot can only be obtained by reducing the value of K_p, but the rise time and settling time will be too large. Thus, the PI controller alone cannot meet the performance requirements given. The preceding results also show that while t_r decreases monotonically with the increase in K_p, the settling time t_s reaches a minimum at around $K_p = 0.03$.

10.3.3 Design of the PID Controller

To design the PID controller, the transfer function in Equation 10-1 is used. We let $K_{p2} = 0.03$, $K_{i2} = 0.003$. The open-loop transfer function of the system with the PID controller is

$$G(s) = G_c(s)G_P(s) = \frac{150(1 + K_{d1}s)(s + 0.1)}{s^2(s + 5)(s + 10)} \qquad (10\text{-}10)$$

To investigate the effect of K_{d1}, we select the Root locus option in tdde-sign, with $K_p = 1$ and $K_i = 0$. This effectively gives the root-locus plot of the characteristic equation using the poles and zeros of the following transfer function:

$$G_{eq}(s) = \frac{K_{d1}s(s + 0.1)}{s^2(s + 5)(s + 10) + 150(s + 0.1)} \qquad (10\text{-}11)$$

which has poles at $s = -11.8376, -0.1035, -1.5295 \pm j3.1478$, and zeros at $s = 0, -0.1, \infty, \infty$. The root locus plot for $K_{d1} > 0$ is shown in Figure 10-5. The intersect of the dominant part of the root loci with the $\zeta = 0.707$ locus yields a value of $K_{d1} = 0.1265$. However, with this value of K_{d1}, the maximum overshoot is still larger than the 4% specified. Increasing the value of K_{d1} would reduce t_r, t_s, and y_{max}. Carrying out several trial-and-error runs for various values of K_{d1}, the following attributes of the step response are obtained for $K_{d1} = 0.3$.

$$t_r = 0.5347 \text{ s}$$

$$t_s = 0.7071 \text{ s}$$

$$y_{max} = 2.7\%$$

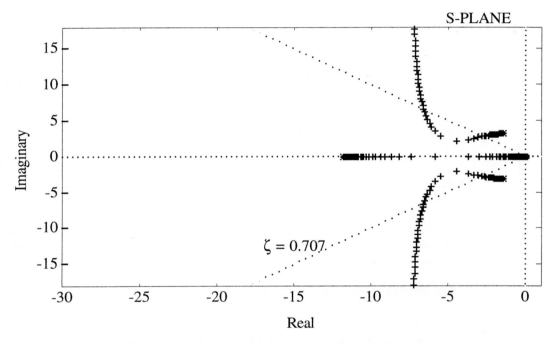

Figure 10-5. Root-locus plot of Equation 10-11 for $K_{d1} > 0$.

Further increasing the value of K_{d1} would cause the settling time to increase.

The unit-step response of the designed system is shown in Figure 10-6.

The values of the PID controller parameters are determined from Equations 10-2, 10-3, and 10-4. We have

$$K_p = K_{p2} + K_{d1}K_{i2} = 0.0309$$

$$K_d = K_{d1}K_{p2} = 0.009$$

$$K_i = K_{i2} = 0.003$$

Chap. 10   **Design of Control Systems**

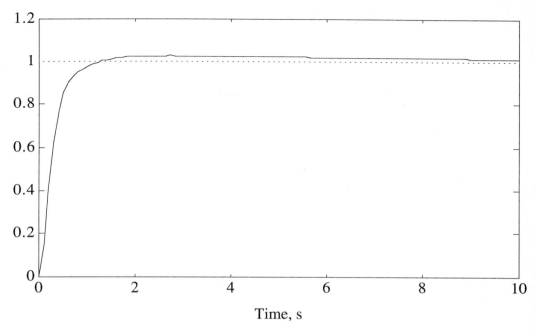

Figure 10-6. Unit-step response of system with PID controller.

10.4 DESIGN OF THE PID CONTROLLER IN THE FREQUENCY DOMAIN

In this section we shall apply `fddesign` in the *CSAD Toolbox* to the design of the PID controller in the frequency domain. Because the time-domain specifications on maximum overshoot, t_r, and t_s give a direct measure of the performance of the unit-step response, designing in the frequency domain has the drudgery of checking the attributes of the step response to see if these specifications are satisfied during the trial-and-error design runs. However, the frequency-domain design gives an alternative with a different perspective to the design problem. Information on bandwidth also gives indication on the robustness and noise-rejection properties of the system.

We shall again use the process transfer function in Equation 10-6 to demonstrate the frequency-domain design.

Entering `fddesign` <CR> at the MATLAB prompt >>, the following responses and data entries occur.

```
Default is: 100
Enter plant numerator > 5000
Default input is: s^2 + 10s^1 + 0
Enter plant denominator > [1 15 50 0]
Controller is: K(1 + aTs)/(1 + Ts)
```

```
K multiplies plant to set DC gain
Enter K [1] > <CR>
Enter a [2] > 1 <CR>
Enter T [0.1] > 1 <CR>
A = 1 gives controller pole-zero cancellation!
1/aT            1
Wm              1
1/T             1
max phase       0
a in dB         0
Press any key to continue . . .
- FDDESIGN OPTIONS -
Controller values
Frequency Response
Lead/Lag math
Goals to meet
Error, steady state
Step Response
Display TF's
Poles and Zeros
New Plant TF
Quit
Option? > f <CR>
Response of K*plant, Lead/Lag, Open-loop, Closed-loop? [0] > k
```

To obtain the open-loop frequency response of the uncompensated system you may choose either K*plant or Open-loop; the latter is acceptable because all the controller parameters are set to unity.

```
Enter START frequency, w = 10^k1, k1 = [-1] > -2 <CR>
Enter END frequency, w = 10^k2, k2 = [1] > 2 <CR>
                  - BODEPLOT OPTIONS -
        Amplitude               Freq range
        Phase                   Time delay
        Both                    New TF
        Zoom in                 Display TF
        Set axes                Margins
        Grid                    Roots
        Hold                    View Data
        Label                   Quit
        Option? > m
        Gain Margin, dB             -16.47
        Phase Crossover, rad/s       7.079
        Phase Margin, degrees      -40.42
        Gain Crossover, rad/s       15.94
        Peak Resonance, dB           4.677
        Peak Resonance, |M_p|        1.7134
        3dB Bandwidth, rad/s        20.01
```

Because the gain and phase margins are negative, the closed-loop system without compensation is unstable. The computed peak resonance should be ignored. Selecting the Amplitude and Phase options, the magnitude and phase plots are obtained as shown in Figure 10-7.

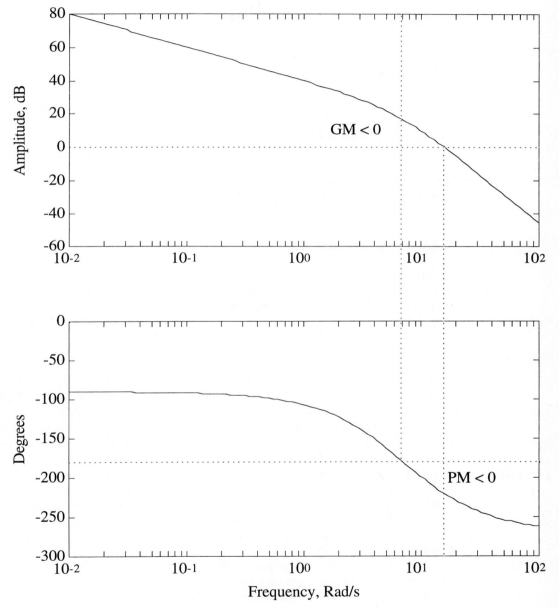

Figure 10-7. Bode plot of $G_p(s) = \dfrac{5000}{s(s + 5)(s + 10)}$.

Returning to the `fddesign` options, selecting `Goals to meet` and setting max % overshoot = 4, t_r = 0.8, and t_s = 0.8, the following estimated requirements on phase margin, M_p and BW are computed:

```
Estimated Minimum Phase Margin required, degrees   65.97
Estimated Maximum Peak Resonance allowed, dB        1
Estimated Minimum 3dB Bandwidth required, rad/s     6.944
```

The requirement on phase margin is determined from Equation 9-9, M_p from Equation 9-4, and bandwidth from Equation 9-6, all with ζ = 0.7156 and ω_n = 7.029 rad/s. Again, these requirements should only be regarded as guidelines toward the design in the frequency domain. Nevertheless, the information is very useful, because it forms the correlation between the time-domain and frequency-domain specifications. The estimated minimuim phase margin required is the most useful, since it indicates that the PID controller must provide an improvement of approximately 106° to the phase margin. The minimum bandwidth is due to the maximum requirements on t_r and t_s.

10.4.1 Design of the PI Controller

To carry out the design using `fddesign`, we can again artificially divide the PID controller into a PD portion and a PI portion, as shown in Equation 10-2. Let us first investigate the PI portion that has the transfer function

$$G_{ci}(s) = K_{p2} + \frac{K_{i2}}{s} = \frac{K_{i2}(1 + K_{p2}s/K_{i2})}{s} \qquad (10\text{-}12)$$

Figure 10-8 shows the Bode plot of $G_{ci}(j\omega)$ for K_{i2} = 0.003 and K_{p2} = 0.03. Notice that the magnitude curve has an attenuation of $20\log_{10}K_{p2}$ at the high frequencies. At low frequencies the PI controller produces a phase lag of up to $-90°$. In general, the attenuation of the magnitude plot will push the gain-crossover of the overall system to a lower frequency, thus realizing a higher phase margin, if the phase lag contributed by the PI controller is not excessive. *The basic principle of the PI control in the frequency domain is to use the high-frequency attenuation of the magnitude characteristics while keeping the affect of the phase lag to a minimum.* Thus, the "trick" is to locate the corner frequency, K_{i2}/K_{p2}, of the PI controller at a frequency far below the dominant poles of the process. Notice that the same guideline was used in the time-domain design demonstrated in Section 10.3.2.

For a minimum phase margin of 66°, Figure 10-7 shows that by modifying the magnitude curve, the gain crossover frequency should be moved from 15.94 rad/s to at least 1.5 rad/s, if the phase curve is not affected by the PI controller. Because the latter is impossible, let us move the gain-crossover frequency to 1 rad/s. Figure 10-7 shows that the magnitude of the PI controller must provide

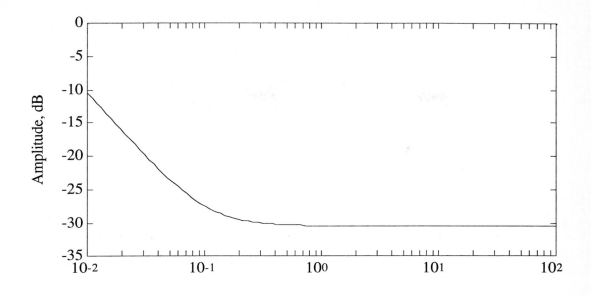

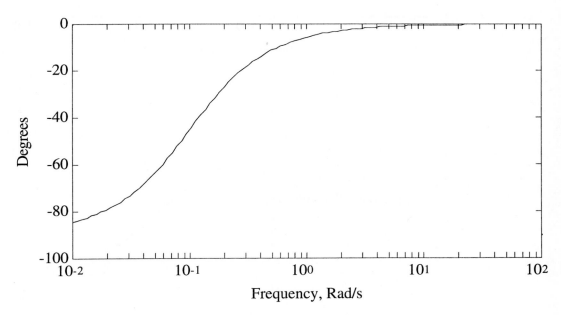

Figure 10-8. Bode plot of PI controller $G_{ci}(s) = K_{p2} + \dfrac{K_{i2}}{s}$, $K_{i2} = 0.003$, $K_{p2} = 0.03$.

an attentuation of approximately -40 dB to realize the new gain crossover. Thus, setting

$$20\log_{10}K_{p2} = -40 \text{ dB} \tag{10-13}$$

Sec. 10.4   Design of PID Controller   **137**

which gives $K_{p2} = 0.01$. Setting $K_{i2}/K_{p2} = 0.1$ arbitrarily far below the dominant pole of $G_p(s)$ at $s = -5$, we have $K_{i2} = 0.001$.

Figure 10-9 shows the Bode plots of the uncompensated plant and the

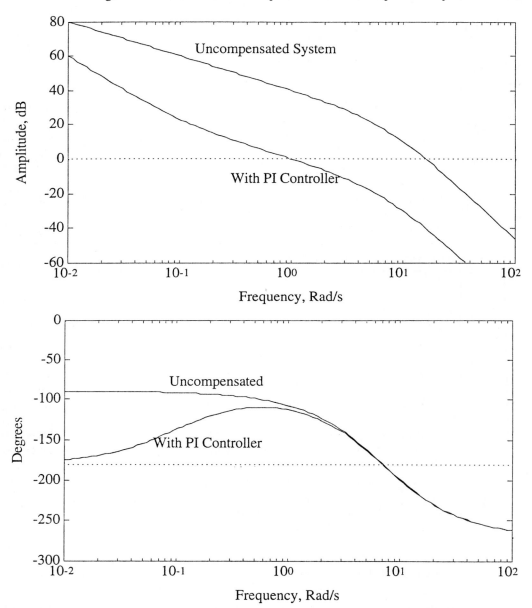

Figure 10-9. Bode plots of compensated and uncompensated system with a PI controller. $G_p(s) = \dfrac{5000}{s(s+5)(s+10)}$; $G_{ci}(s) = 0.01 + 0.001/s$.

Chap. 10   Design of Control Systems

compensated system with the preceding PI-controller parameters. The `Margins` of the compensated system are

```
Gain Margin, dB          23.26
Phase Crossover, rad/s   6.971
Phase Margin, degrees    67.45
Gain Crossover, rad/s    0.9825
Peak Resonance, dB       0.7077
3dB Bandwidth, rad/s     1.515
```

Notice that although the required phase margin is satisfied, the PI controller has reduced the bandwidth of the system substantially.

Returning to `fddesign` from `bplot` by entering `Quit`, we can show by selecting `Step response` and then `Attributes` that the maximum overshoot with the PI controller designed earlier is still 8.4%, and t_r and t_s are all larger than the desired values. This means that the guideline value on minimum-phase margin required of 66° is still not adequate. More serious is that the maximum overshoot, and the response times requirements cannot be satisfied by the PI controller alone, because pushing the gain crossover to a still lower frequency would reduce the bandwidth still lower, resulting in a slower response. This is the same conclusion reached in the time-domain design.

10.4.2 Design of the PD Controller

The PD portion of the PID controller described in Equation 10-2 is written

$$G_{cd}(s) = 1 + K_{d1}s \qquad (10\text{-}14)$$

The Bode plot of $G_{cd}(j\omega)$ is shown in Figure 10-10 for $K_{d1} = 0.03$, which is arbitrarily chosen. Notice that the magnitude of $G_{cd}(j\omega)$ increases with a slope of 20 dB per decade of ω, starting from the corner frequency $\omega = 1/K_{d1}$. The phase of $G_{cd}(j\omega)$ increases from 0 to 90° as ω increases.

The principle of designing the PD controller is to make use of the positive phase characteristics of the controller to improve the phase margin, while keeping the adverse effect of the magnitude characteristics to a minimum. However, the positive magnitude of $G_{cd}(j\omega)$ will shift the gain crossover to a higher frequency, thus reducing the effectiveness of the phase lead. We can immediately draw the conclusion that the PD controller cannot meet the time-domain specifications, because we have established that the net increase in phase required is 106°, and the maximum phase lead the controller can provide absolutely is 90°.

To show the design principle of the PD controller, Figure 10-11 shows the Bode plot of the open-loop transfer function with the PD controller, with $K_{d1} = 0.3$.

$$G_{cd}(s)G_p(s) = \frac{5000(1 + 0.3s)}{s(s + 5)(s + 10)} \qquad (10\text{-}15)$$

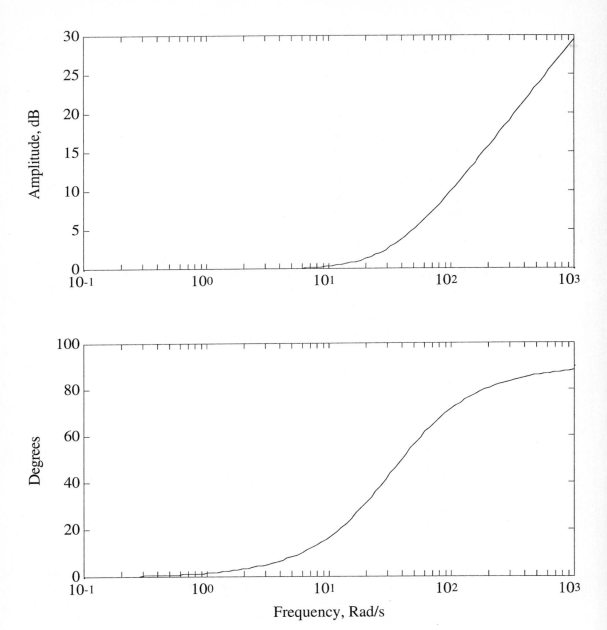

Figure 10-10. Bode plot of PD controller $G_{cd}(s) = 1 + K_{d1}s$, $K_{d1} = 0.03$.

Notice that even though the phase of the compensated system is increased by the PD controller, the gain crossover is also moved to a higher frequency, thus reducing the net increase in the phase margin. The following tabulation shows that $K_{d1} = 0.25$ is close to being optimum from the phase margin and M_p

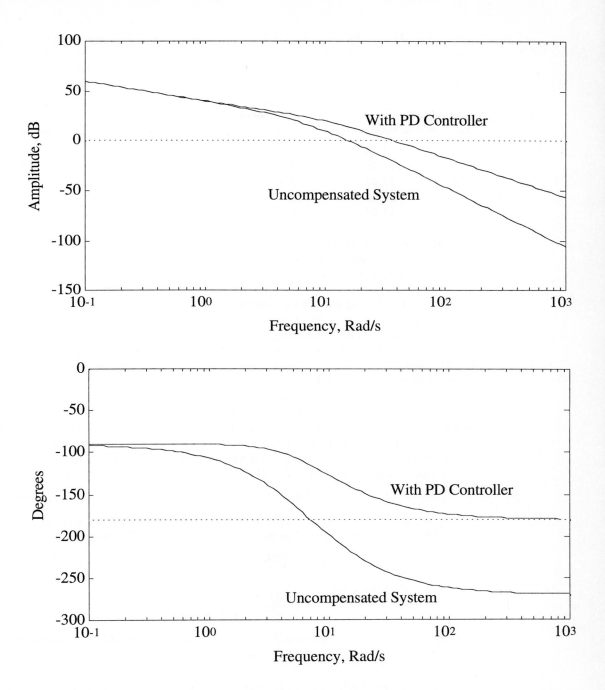

Figure 10-11. Bode plots of compensated and uncompensated systems with PD controller. $G_p(s) = \dfrac{5000}{s(s + 5)(s + 10)}$ $(G_{ci}(s) = 1 + 0.03s)$.

Sec. 10.4   Design of PID Controller

standpoint. The accuracy of computing M_p is again subject to the problem of finding the peak value with a finite number of data points. Increasing or decreasing K_{d1} from this value would reduce the phase margin. The bandwidth is increased by the PD controller and would have no difficulty in exceeding the 6.944 rad/s set by the goals guideline.

K_{d1}	PHASE MARGIN (deg)	M_p (dB)	BW (rad/s)	GAIN CROSSOVER FREQ. (rad/s)
0.1	12.76	13.06	34.48	22.08
0.25	17.76	10.17	54.13	34.61
0.28	17.47	10.07	57.33	36.71
0.3	17.24	11.43	59.4	38.02
0.5	14.92	11.48	77.06	49.44

In general, PD control is more effective when the uncompensated system is not too severely unstable, and the slope of the phase characteristics near the gain crossover is not too large.

10.4.3 The Design of the PID Controller

The conclusion from the preceding design trials is that the given system should be compensated by a PID controller. The PI portion improves the phase margin and M_p, and the PD portion improves or maintains the bandwidth besides contributing to improved stability.

We can set K_{d1} to 0.3, although the optimal value is near 0.25 when the PD controller is acting alone, and start with the Bode plot of Figure 10-11. The system with the PD controller has a phase margin of 17.24°. Let us set our target at 70°. From Figure 10-11, to realize a phase margin of 70°, the gain crossover should be moved from 38.02 rad/s to approximately 6 rad/s, which requires an attenuation of approximately -26 dB. The value of K_{p2} is found from

$$20\log_{10} K_{p2} = -26 \text{ dB} \qquad (10\text{-}16)$$

Solving for K_{p2} we have $K_{p2} = 0.05$. Now setting $K_{i2}/K_{p2} = 0.1$, we have $K_{i2} = 0.005$. The open-loop transfer function of the compensated system is written

$$
\begin{aligned}
G_c(s)G_p(s) &= \frac{5000K_{p2}(1 + K_{d1}s)(s + K_{i2}/K_{p2})}{s^2(s + 5)(s + 10)} \\
&= \frac{250(1 + 0.3s)(s + 0.1)}{s^2(s + 5)(s + 10)}
\end{aligned}
\qquad (10\text{-}16)
$$

The Bode plot of the compensated system with the PID controller is shown in Figure 10-12. The performance data are

```
Gain margin, dB          inf
Phase Crossover, rad/s   inf
Phase Margin, degrees    70.35
Gain Crossover, rad/s    5.60
```

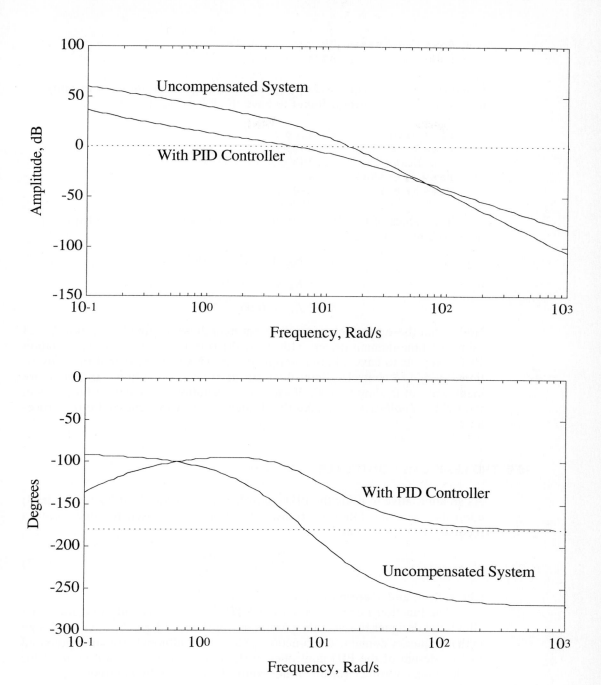

Figure 10-12. Bode plots of uncompensated and compensated system with PID controller. $G_p(s) = \dfrac{5000}{s(s + 5)(s + 10)}$ $G_c(s) = 0.0502 + 0.015s + 0.005/s$.

Sec. 10.4   Design of PID Controller

143

```
Peak Resonance, dB          0.1445
3 dB Bandwidth, rad/s       8.714
```

Using the `Step response` option of `fddesign`, the unit-step response of the compensated system is found to have the following attributes:

```
Delay Time        0.1668
Rise Time         0.2813
Settling time     0.303
Max % Overshoot   1.6
Time at Max       2.222
```

The values of the PID controller parameters are determined from Equations 10-2 to 10-4. We have

$$K_p = K_{p2} + K_{d1}K_{i2} = 0.0502$$

$$K_d = K_{d1}K_{p2} = 0.015$$

$$K_i = K_{i2} = 0.005$$

Notice that these parameters are different than those obtained in Section 10.3.3 using the time-domain design. However, the compensated system in Equation 10-16 happens to have a better step response. This just shows that the conventional design of control systems does not have unique solutions, and there are many ways of leading to a set of satisfactory solutions. The design functions in the *CSAD Toolbox* simply take the drudgery out of the trial-and-error procedures.

10.5 THE LEAD-LAG CONTROLLER

As an alternative to using the PID controller, a first-order lead-lag (or lag-lead) controller with the following transfer function can be used to compensate a feedback control system.

$$G_c(s) = K \frac{1 + aTs}{1 + Ts} \tag{10-17}$$

where K, a, and T are positive real constants.

The function `fddesign` in the *CSAD Toolbox* has a built-in feature that allows the designer to select the parameters of the lead-lag controller for design in the frequency domain. The function `tddesign`, although primarily prepared for the design of the PID controller in the time domain, can still be used for the lead-lag controller (or any other controller), simply by entering $G_c(s)G_p(s)$ as the plant transfer function.

Before embarking on the design with the lead-lag controller, it is informative to investigate its properties in the time and frequency domains. Figure 10-13 shows the pole-zero configurations of $G_c(s)$ of Equation 10-17 for $a < 1$ and

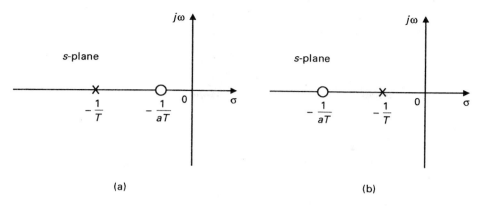

Figure 10-13. Pole-zero configuration of lead-lag controller. $G_c(s) = (1 + aTs)/(1 + Ts)$. (a) $a > 1$. (b) $a < 1$.

$a > 1$. Figure 10-14 shows the Bode diagrams of $G_c(s)$ for the two cases of a. As shown in Figure 10-14, when a is greater than one, the phase of $G_c(j\omega)$ is positive for all ω. When a is less than one, the phase of $G_c(j\omega)$ is negative for all ω. Thus, when $a < 1$ the controller is called a *phase-lag* controller. When $a > 1$ the controller is called a *phase-lead* controller. For design purposes, the gain K in Equation 10-17 may be set to unity, because the loop gain of the system may be adjusted by varying the gain of the plant transfer function.

10.5.1 Design of the Phase-Lead Controller in the Time Domain

From the pole-zero configuration in Figure 10-13(a) we see that when $a > 1$ the zero of the phase-lead controller is to the right of the pole. From the time-domain standpoint, the zero at $-1/aT$ will cause the root loci of the plant to be drawn to the left in the s-plane. The pole at $-1/T$ will cause the root loci to be pushed to the right. Because the zero is closer to the $j\omega$-axis, it has a more dominant effect.

The strategy of designing the phase-lead controller in the time domain is to artificially use only the numerator polynomial $(1 + aTs)$ first. Because the denominator polynomial $(1 + Ts)$ would only cause the system stability to deteriorate, using only $(1 + aTs)$ term and finding the optimal value of aT is the best that can be obtained for the system. To complete the design, we should set T to a very small value, so that the pole at $-1/T$ is far to the left in the s-plane. For the system described by Equation 10-6 with $K = 5000$, selecting $aT = 0.25$ and $T = 0.001$ will yield a step response very close to that shown in Figure 10-3 (maximum overshoot = 62.6%).

Let us use an illustrative example on a system that will be effective with the phase-lead controller. A sun-seeker system has the plant transfer function

$$G_p(s) = \frac{2500}{s(s + 25)} \tag{10-18}$$

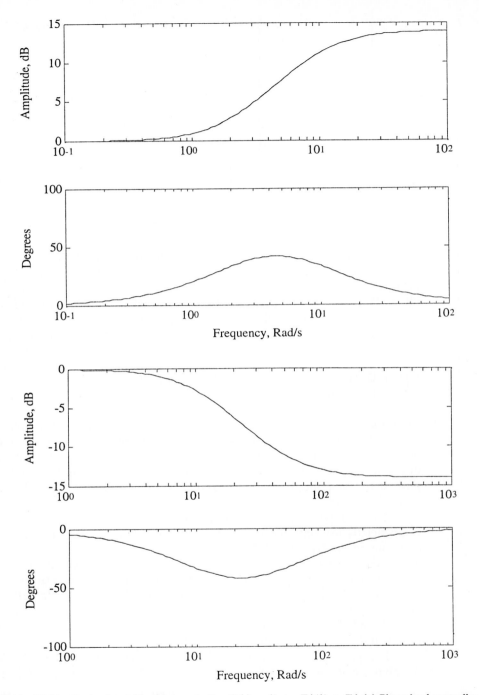

Figure 10-14. Bode plots of lead-lag controller $G_c(s) = (1 + aTs)/(1 + Ts)$ (a) Phase-lead controller $(a > 0)$. (b) Phase-lag controller $(a < 0)$.

Chap. 10   **Design of Control Systems**

We can show that the uncompensated system has a maximum overshoot of 44.4%.

Let the design specifications be

$$t_r < 0.05 \text{ s}$$

$$t_s < 0.05 \text{ s}$$

$$\text{maximum overshoot} < 2\%$$

Let us select the phase-lead controller in Equation 10-17 with $a > 1$. First, we apply only the numerator factor of Equation 10-17 to the system, with $K = 1$. Entering the system parameters in tddesign, we get by a few trial-and-error runs from which we select $aT = 0.035$, resulting in a system with the following attributes:

$$t_r = 0.02308 \text{ s}$$

$$t_s = 0.02843 \text{ s}$$

$$\text{maximum \% overshoot} = 0.9$$

Next we restore the denominator term in Equation 10-17, and select $T = 0.002$. The transfer function of the phase-lead controller is

$$G_c(s) = \frac{1 + 0.035s}{1 + 0.002s} \tag{10-19}$$

The attributes of the step response of the system with the phase-lead controller are:

$$t_r = 0.01923 \text{ s}$$

$$t_s = 0.02421 \text{ s}$$

$$\text{maximum \% overshoot} = 1.3$$

It should be pointed out that the value of T should not be excessively small, or the value of a will be too large for practical realization.

10.5.2 Design of the Phase-Lead Controller in the Frequency Domain

Design of the phase-lead controller in Equation 10-17 can be carried out using fddesign. The function features the controller connected in series with the plant transfer function, so that all one has to do is select the parameters a and T. With reference to the Bode plot of the phase-lead controller in Figure 10-14(a), we see that the magnitude curve has a gain of $20\log_{10}a$ dB at high frequencies. The phase has a peak value ϕ_m that is related to a by the equation,

$$\phi_m = \sin^{-1}\left(\frac{a - 1}{a + 1}\right) \tag{10-20}$$

The maximum phase ϕ_m occurs at the frequency,

$$\omega_m = \frac{1}{\sqrt{a}\ T} \qquad (10\text{-}21)$$

Given the value of ϕ_m the corresponding value of a is obtained from Equation 10-20,

$$a = \frac{1 + \sin \phi_m}{1 - \sin \phi_m} \qquad (10\text{-}22)$$

Because the phase-lead controller features a positive phase characteristic, and a maximum phase ϕ_m, the principle of design is to make use of ϕ_m to improve the phase margin, while keeping the effect of the magnitude to a minimum. Because the positive phase is accompanied by a positive gain, the latter will move the gain-crossover point to a higher frequency, making the phase lead less effective. The design steps involve first the determination of the value of a to realize the amount of phase required to achieve a certain desired phase margin, and then the value of T so that ω_m is located at the best place to maximize the phase lead effect.

The Lead/lag math option of fddesign computes the value of a using Equation 10-22 once the value of ϕ_m is given. The value of a is also computed for the phase-lag controller but is of no concern to us at this point.

If the design calls for the realization of a desired phase margin, the value of ϕ_m is determined from how much additional phase is needed to raise the phase margin from the uncompensated value to the desired value. The value of ω_m is set at the frequency where the magnitude curve of the uncompensated $G_p(j\omega)$ is $-10\log_{10}a$ dB (half the value of the maximum gain of the phase-lead controller). This will locate ω_m at the new gain crossover of the compensated system.

Let us design a phase-lead controller for the system with the plant transfer function given by Equation 10-18 so that the unit-step response has the attributes: $t_r < 0.05$ s, $t_s < 0.05$ s, and maximum overshoot $< 2\%$. Entering these requirements in the Goals to meet option in fddesign, the following requirements on the frequency response are given:

```
Estimated Minimum Phase Margin required, deg       69
Estimated Maximum Peak Resonance allowed, dB        1
Estimated Minimum 3dB Bandwidth required, rad/s    97.16
```

Because the uncompensated system has a phase margin of 28°, the additional phase lead that must be provided by the controller is 41°. Let the value of ϕ_m be 45°. Lead/Lag math (or Equation 10-22) gives $a = 5.828$. From the magnitude plot of $G_c(j\omega)$ ω_m should be set at the pont where $|G_c(j\omega)| = 10\log_{10}(5.828) = -7.655$ dB. Thus, using the magnitude plot of $G_c(j\omega)$ and the "View data" option of fddesign, ω_m is found to be at 75 rad/s. Using Equation 10-21, T

is found to be 0.0055, and thus, $aT = 0.0322$. The transfer function of the phase-lead controller is

$$G_c(s) = \frac{1 + 0.0322s}{1 + 0.0055s} \qquad (10\text{-}23)$$

However, the compensated system has a phase margin of only 63.24°, and the unit-step response has a maximum overshoot of 7.5%. This means that we must select a larger value for ϕ_m. After a couple of trial-and-error runs, the acceptable value of ϕ_m is finally found to be 60°. The corresponding phase-lead controller transfer function is

$$G_c(s) = \frac{1 + 0.03857s}{1 + 0.00276s} \qquad (10\text{-}24)$$

The compensated system now has a phase margin of 75° and a BW of 126.6 rad/s. The attributes of the unit-step response are

$$t_r = 0.01697 \text{ s}$$

$$t_s = 0.02287 \text{ s}$$

$$\text{maximum \% overshoot} = 0.4$$

Notice that the phase-lead controller in Equation 10-24 is different than that in Equation 10-19, which is obtained using the time-domain design approach. However, both controllers meet the design specifications.

10.5.3 Design of the Phase-Lag Controller in the Time Domain

When the value of a is less then unity, the controller described by Equation 10-17 is a phase-lag controller. The pole-zero configuration of Figure 10-13(b) shows that the pole at $-1/T$ is always to the right of the zero at $-1/aT$. It would seem that the phase-lag controller is always detrimental to system stability, because as explained in Section 10.5.1 the pole may cause the root loci of the characteristic equation roots to be pushed toward the right-half s-plane. However, just as in the PI controller design, by properly placing the location of the poles and zeros of $G_c(s)$, the phase-lag controller can have a wider range of effectiveness on system stability than the phase-lead controller. Figure 10-14 shows that the magnitude plot of the phase-lag controller has an attenuation of $20\log_{10}a$ at high frequencies. This will always cause the bandwidth of the compensated system to be lower. Therefore, the disadvantage of the phase-lag controller is that the relative stability of the compensated system is improved at the expense of rise and settling times.

The principle of designing the phase-lag controller can be explained by referring to the open-loop transfer function of the compensated system,

$$G(s) = G_c(s)G_p(s) = \frac{1 + aTs}{1 + Ts} G_p(s) \qquad (10\text{-}25)$$

If the value of T is large, so that the pole at $-1/T$ is very close to the origin in the s-plane, and the zero at $-1/aT$ is placed very close to the pole, $G(s)$ in Equation 10-25 can be approximated as

$$G(s) = G_c(s)G_p(s) \cong aG_p(s) \qquad (10\text{-}26)$$

at relatively high frequencies. Thus, the effective of the phase-lag controller on the transient response is to multiply the loop gain by a factor of a (< 1). The value of a is then selected so that the desired transient performance is achieved.

To illustrate the design of the phase-lag controller in the time-domain, let us use the plant transfer function in Equation 10-6 with $K = 5000$. The closed-loop system without compensation is unstable.

The design of the phase-lag controller in the time domain may be carried out using `tddesign` in the *CSAD Toolbox*. The parameters of the PID controller in `tddesign` are selected as $K_p = 1$, $K_d = 0$, and $K_i = 0$.

The root-locus plot of the uncompensated system with $K = 5000$, and the transfer function in Equation 10-26 is shown in Figure 10-15. Let us arbitrarily choose the $\zeta = 0.707$ point as the target for operation. Choosing a relative damping of 0.707 will not give a minimum value for the maximum overshoot, but is generally thought of as a preferred choice for all-around performance with respect to maximum overshoot and response time. Because the lead-lag controller of Equation 10-6 is essentially a "one-dimensional" controller, in general, it cannot satisfy stringent requirements on both the maximum overshoot and response times simultaneously. Figure 10-15 shows that for $\zeta = 0.707$ the value of a is approximately 0.0163. Note that this corresponds to setting $K = 81.5$ ($= 5000 \times 0.0163$) in the original system.

Setting $a = 0.0163$, the following tabulation indicates the various attributes of the step response when T varies.

$a = 0.0163$

T	aT	MAXIMUM % OVERSHOOT	t_r (s)	t_s (s)
100	1.63	36	0.6222	3.396
500	8.15	11.5	0.7629	4.444
1,000	16.3	7.9	0.7941	2.424
5,000	81.5	4.9	0.8219	1.111
10,000	163	4.5	0.8255	1.111

We can see that as the value of T increases, the maximum overshoot decreases, because the effects of the pole at $s = -1/T$ diminish. As T increases, t_s decreases, but t_r increases. We must point out that in practice extremely large values of T may be difficult to realize physically by hardware.

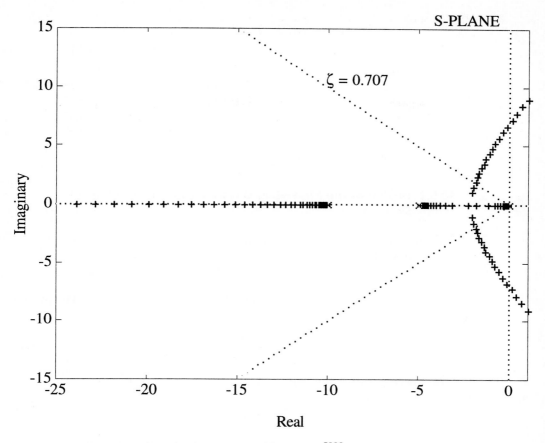

Figure 10-15. Root-locus plot of $G(s) = \dfrac{5000a}{s(s+5)(s+10)}$ for $0 < a < \infty$.

Let us investigate the case when the value of a lies on either side of 0.0163. The results are tabulated below for $a = 0.01$ and $a = 0.02$.

$a = 0.01$

T	aT	MAXIMUM % OVERSHOOT	t_r (s)	t_s (s)
100	1.0	51.1	0.784	6.431
500	5.0	15.1	1.166	8.283
1,000	10.0	8.3	1.295	8.889
5,000	50.0	1.9	1.467	2.02
10,000	100.0	1.0	1.495	2.121

$a = 0.02$

T	aT	MAXIMUM % OVERSHOOT	t_r (s)	t_s (s)
100	2.0	33	0.5547	3.01
500	10.0	13.7	0.6375	2.323
1,000	20.0	11.1	0.6517	2.02
5,000	100.0	9.0	0.6637	1.818
10,000	200.0	8.7	0.6653	1.818

10.5.4 Design of the Phase-Lag Controller in the Frequency Domain

As shown in Figure 10-14(b), the phase-lag controller in Equation 10-6 has an attenuation of

$$\text{attenuation} = 20\log_{10}a \text{ dB } (a < 1) \tag{10-27}$$

at the high frequencies, and a negative phase for all frequencies. The maximum phase is

$$\phi_m = \frac{a - 1}{a + 1} (a < 1) \tag{10-28}$$

and it occurs at the frequency,

$$\omega_m = \frac{1}{\sqrt{a}\, T} \tag{10-29}$$

Unlike the phase-lead compensation that uses the maximum phase-lead of the controller, phase-lag compensation uses the attenuation of the controller at high frequencies. If the phase characteristics of the uncompensated system have a negative slope with respect to ω, and it usually has in most control systems, moving the gain crossover to a lower frequency would increase the phase margin. Thus, the design strategy with the phase-lag controller is to use the high-frequency attenuation property to lower the gain crossover of the plant while keeping the effect of the phase lag to a minimum. The latter can be achieved

When $a = 0.01$, the corresponding damping ratio is greater than 0.707, so the overshoot should be less and response time should be slower. The above results show that this is true for t_r and t_s for all values of T used. However, the maximum overshoot is higher for low values of T. For higher values of T, the maximum overshoot decreases dramatically, as it should be.

When $a = 0.02$, the corresponding damping ratio is greater than 0.707, so that the maximum overshoot should be greater than the $a = 0.0163$ case, and the response times should be faster. The preceding tabulated results show that t_r and t_s are indeed shorter for all the T's used. However, the maximum

overshoot is slightly lower when T is relatively small. When T is larger, the maximum overshoot is greater than the $a = 0.0163$ case.
by placing the upper corner frequency of the controller, $1/aT$ far below the poles of the plant.

Design of the phase-lag controller in the frequency domain can be carried out using fddesign in the *CSAD Toolbox*. The function features the controller connected in series with the plant transfer function, so that all one has to do is select the parameters a and T. The Lead/lag math option in fddesign gives the corresponding value of a once the desired amount of attenuation in dB is entered, using the relationship in Equation 10-27.

To illustrate the principles of designing the phase-lag controller using fddesign, let us again consider the plant transfer function in Equation 10-6 with $K = 5000$. The Bode plot of the plant is already shown in Figure 10-7. The "margins" of the uncompensated system have been listed in Section 10.4. Of interest is that the uncompensated system is unstable and has a bandwidth of 20 rad/s. The bandwidth information is important, because the phase-lag controller cannot realize a step response requirement that would correspond to a bandwidth requirement greater than 20 rad/s. For example, entering the following performance requirements under Goals to meet:

```
Enter Max % Overshoot [0] > 2
Enter Min Rise Time [100] > 0.05
enter Min Settling Time [100] > 0.05
```

and the function returns:

```
Estimated Minimum Phase Margin required, degrees    69
Estimated Maximum Peak Resonance allowed, dB         1
Estimated Minimum 3dB Bandwidth required, rad/s    97.16
```

Although it is possible to realize the requirements on phase margin and M_p, the minimum requirement on bandwidth cannot be achieved with the phase-lag controller for this system, because the phase-lag controller will always reduce the bandwidth from the uncompensated value of 20 rad/s. From the information obtained in the time-domain design discussed in the last section, we enter the following performance requirements under Goals to meet:

```
Enter Max % Overshoot [0] > 2
Enter Min Rise Time [100] > 2
Enter Min Settling Time [100] > 1.5
```

and the function returns:

```
Estimated Minimum Phase Margin required, degrees    69
Estimated Maximum Peak Resonance allowed, dB         1
Estimated Minimum 3dB Bandwidth required, rad/s    3.239
```

Sec. 10.5   The Lead-Lag Controller

Thus, the last set of requirements on t_r and t_s are more reasonable for the phase-lag controller to achieve.

Let us carry out the design with the last set of performance requirements. First we refer to the Bode plot in Figure 10-7 to find the required amount of attenuation of the magnitude plot to realize the desired phase margin. Because the phase lag property will always affect the phase margin adversely, let us add a safety margin by requiring that the compensated system should have a phase margin of 74°. From Figure 10-7 we observe that the gain crossover must be moved from 15.94 rad/s to 0.95 rad/s at which the magnitude of $G_p(j\omega)$ is 40 dB. These values can be more accurately determined with the View data option.

To move the gain crossover to 0.95 rad/s, we need an attenuation of -40 dB from the phase-lag controller. Thus, a is determined from Equation 10-27,

$$a = 10^{-40/20} = 10^{-2} = 0.01 \tag{10-30}$$

Note that this value of a was one of the values we selected in the time-domain design, and the corresponding relative damping ratio is slightly below 0.707. Selecting a proper large value for T would complete the design. To investigate the effects of T, the following results are obtained:

T	aT	ΦM °	GM dB	PHASE CO rad/s	GAIN CO rad/s	M_p dB	BW rad/s	% Max OVERSHOOT	t_r s	t_s s
100	1	30.56	20.46	5.933	1.239	6.106	2.165	51.1	0.784	6.431
500	5	61.78	22.99	6.862	0.9965	1.328	1.612	15.1	1.166	8.283
1,000	10	67.51	23.27	6.972	0.9825	0.6993	1.514	8.3	1.295	8.889
5,000	50	72.19	23.48	7.058	0.9777	0.1541	1.422	1.9	1.467	2.02
10,000	100	72.77	23.5	7.068	0.9776	0.0793	1.409	1.0	1.495	2.121

The Bode plots of the uncompensated plant transfer function and the phase-lag compensated system with $a = 0.01$ and $T = 5000$ are shown in Figure 10-16. The maximum overshoot of the step response is 1.9%, but the rise and settling times are 1.467 and 2.02 s, respectively. The bandwidth of the system is reduced to 1.422 rad/s.

10.6 STATE-FEEDBACK CONTROL: POLE-PLACEMENT DESIGN

When a linear system is described by state equations, a closed-loop control system may be formed by feeding back the state variables through constant gains to form the control signal. Let an nth-order linear time-invariant system be represented by the following state equation:

$$\frac{d\mathbf{x}(t)}{dt} = \mathbf{Ax}(t) + \mathbf{B}u(t) \tag{10-31}$$

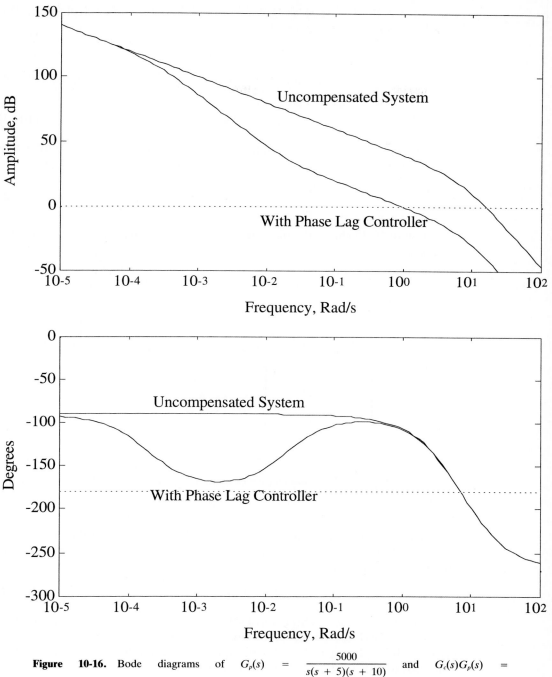

Figure 10-16. Bode diagrams of $G_p(s) = \dfrac{5000}{s(s + 5)(s + 10)}$ and $G_c(s)G_p(s) = \dfrac{5000(1 + 50s)}{s(s + 5)(s + 10)(1 + 5000s)}$.

where $\mathbf{x}(t)$ is the $n \times 1$ state vector, and $u(t)$ is the scalar control input. The state-feedback control is defined as

$$u(t) = -\mathbf{K}\mathbf{x}(t) + r(t) \qquad (10\text{-}32)$$

where $r(t)$ is the reference input, and $\mathbf{K}$ is the $1 \times n$ feedback matrix that can be expressed as

$$\mathbf{K} = [k_1 \ k_2 \cdots k_n] \qquad (10\text{-}33)$$

where $k_1, k_2, \ldots, k_n$ are constant gains. Substituting Equation 10-32 into Equation 10-31, the closed-loop system is represented by the state equation

$$\frac{d\mathbf{x}(t)}{dt} = (\mathbf{A} - \mathbf{BK})\mathbf{x}(t) + \mathbf{B}r(t) \qquad (10\text{-}34)$$

Figure 10-17 shows the block diagram of the closed-loop system with state feedback.

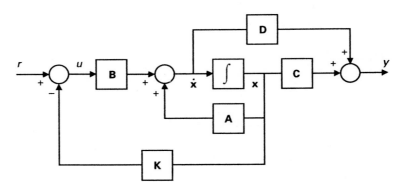

Figure 10-17. Block diagram of control system with state feedback.

The feedback matrix $\mathbf{K}$ can be designed by requiring that the eigenvalues of $\mathbf{A} - \mathbf{BK}$ take on certain specific values. In other words, the roots of the characteristic equation

$$|\lambda\mathbf{I} - \mathbf{A} + \mathbf{BK}| = 0 \qquad (10\text{-}35)$$

takes on specific values. This control strategy is known as *pole-placement design*.

The analytical problem of the pole-placement design using state feedback involves the equating of like coefficients of Equation 10-35 and the equation that corresponds to the desired eigenvalues.

We must investigate under what condition solution to the elements of $\mathbf{K}$ exists when the eigenvalues of the closed-loop system are arbitrarily assigned.

Consider that the coefficient matrices are expressed in CCF, that is,

$$
\mathbf{A} = \begin{bmatrix}
0 & 1 & 0 & \cdots & 0 \\
0 & 0 & 1 & \cdots & 0 \\
0 & 0 & 0 & \cdots & 0 \\
\vdots & \vdots & \vdots & \vdots\vdots & \vdots \\
0 & 0 & 0 & \cdots & 1 \\
-a_1 & -a_2 & -a_3 & \cdots & -a_n
\end{bmatrix}
\qquad
\mathbf{B} = \begin{bmatrix}
0 \\
0 \\
0 \\
\vdots \\
0 \\
1
\end{bmatrix}
\qquad (10\text{-}36)
$$

Then, the coefficient matrix of the closed-loop system with state feedback is

$$
\mathbf{A} - \mathbf{BK} = \begin{bmatrix}
0 & 1 & 0 & \cdots & 0 \\
0 & 0 & 1 & \cdots & 0 \\
\vdots & \vdots & \vdots & \vdots\vdots & \vdots \\
0 & 0 & 0 & \cdots & 1 \\
-a_1 - k_1 & -a_2 - k_2 & -a_3 - k_3 & \cdots & -a_n - k_n
\end{bmatrix}
\qquad (10\text{-}37)
$$

The characteristic equation of $\mathbf{A} - \mathbf{BK}$ is

$$
|\lambda\mathbf{I} - \mathbf{BK}| = \lambda^n + (a_n + k_n)\lambda^{n-1} +
$$

$$
\cdots + (a_2 + k_2)\lambda + (a_1 + k_1) = 0 \qquad (10\text{-}38)
$$

It is apparent that by equating the n coefficients of the last equation to those of the equation that corresponds to the desired eigenvalues, we will get n linearly independent equations with the gains $k_1, k_2, \ldots, k_n$ all isolated. This guarantees unique solutions for the feedback gains.

The conclusion is that if the system is modeled in CCF, then the eigenvalues of the closed-loop system can be arbitrarily assigned, and unique solutions to $\mathbf{K}$ are guaranteed. Because CCF implies complete controllability, we can say that if the pair $[\mathbf{A}, \mathbf{B}]$ is controllable, then the closed-loop system with state feedback defined by Equation 10-32 can have arbitrarily assigned eigenvalues, and the solution to $\mathbf{K}$ is unique.

As an illustrative example to state-feedback control, let us consider that the system described by Equation 10-31 has the following coefficient matrices.

$$
\mathbf{A} = \begin{bmatrix}
1 & 0 & 0 \\
-1 & 0 & 2 \\
0 & -1 & 1
\end{bmatrix}
\qquad
\mathbf{B} = \begin{bmatrix}
1 \\
0 \\
0
\end{bmatrix}
\qquad (10\text{-}36)
$$

We can show that $\mathbf{A}$ and $\mathbf{B}$ are completely controllable. Let the desired eigenvalues of the closed-loop system be at $s = -2, -1$, and -1; that is, the desired closed-loop characteristic equation is

$$
s^3 + 4s^2 + 5s + 2 = 0 \qquad (10\text{-}37)
$$

The feedback matrix $\mathbf{K}$ for the third-order system is written

$$\mathbf{K} = [k_1 \quad k_2 \quad k_3] \tag{10-38}$$

Equation 10-35 is written as

$$|\lambda\mathbf{I} - \mathbf{A} + \mathbf{BK}| = \begin{vmatrix} \lambda - 1 + k_1 & k_2 & k_3 \\ 1 & \lambda & -2 \\ 0 & 1 & \lambda - 1 \end{vmatrix}$$

$$= \lambda^3 + (k_1 - 2)\lambda^2 + (3 - k_1 - k_2)\lambda \tag{10-39}$$

$$+ 2k_1 + k_2 + k_3 - 2$$

Now equating like coefficients of Equations 10-37 and 10-39, we have

$$k_1 - 2 = 4$$

$$3 - k_1 - k_2 = 5 \tag{10-40}$$

$$2k_1 + k_2 + k_3 - 2 = 2$$

Solving these equations, we have

$$k_1 = 6 \qquad k_2 = -8 \qquad k_3 = 0 \tag{10-41}$$

The function $\mathtt{svstuff}$ in the *CSAD Toolbox* contains a feature that solves the state-feedback design. After entering the system parameters, either in state variable form or transfer function form, the $\mathtt{State\ feedback}$ option may be selected. The following dialog ensues:

```
Include Integral Control of output? (y/n) [n] > <CR>
Enter vector of 3 desired pole locations > [-2 -1 -1] <CR>
State-Feedback Vector K is:
    6    -8    0
```

To see the $\mathbf{A}$ matrix of the system with state feedback (or $\mathbf{A} - \mathbf{BK}$), you should select the $\mathtt{Display\ A,B,C,D}$ option again. In addition to the $\mathbf{A}$, $\mathbf{B}$, $\mathbf{C}$, $\mathbf{D}$ of the open-loop system, the $\mathbf{A}$ matrix of the closed-loop system is displayed as

```
System with state feedback.
A matrix is:
   -5    8    0
   -1    0    2
    0   -1    1
```

Selecting $\mathtt{Response\ to\ step}$ will get you the step response of either the system with or without state feedback.

As another illustrative example, the following plant transfer function is entered as $N(s)/D(s)$ in $\mathtt{svstuff}$.

$$G_p(s) = \frac{N(s)}{D(s)} = \frac{1}{s^2(s+1)} \tag{10-42}$$

This is a type 2 system, so the steady-state error of a conventional feedback system should have zero steady-state error when the system is subject to a step input.

The state-variable representation of the system in CCF is

$$\mathbf{A} = \begin{bmatrix} 0 & 1 & 0 \\ 0 & 0 & 1 \\ 0 & 0 & -1 \end{bmatrix} \quad \mathbf{B} = \begin{bmatrix} 0 \\ 0 \\ 1 \end{bmatrix} \quad \mathbf{C} = \begin{bmatrix} 1 & 0 & 0 \end{bmatrix} \tag{10-43}$$

Selecting State feedback without integral control of output from the svstuff options, we have the following dialog and results:

```
Include Integral Control of output? (y/n) [n] > <CR>
Enter vector of 3 desired pole locations > [-1 -1+2*i -1-2*i] <CR>
State Feedback Vector K is:
     3   3   0
```

Selecting the Display A,B,C,D option again, the **A** matrix of the closed-loop system is displayed as:

```
System with state feedback.
A matrix is:
      0    1    0
      0    0    1
     -5   -7   -3
```

Problem 10-11 requires that the system be represented in OCF, and the state-feedback design is to be repeated. Comment on why the solutions for **K** are different.

If we choose the Response to step option, with the designed state feedback the unit-step response is shown to have no overshoot, but the final value is 0.2. Thus, the system has a steady-state error of 80% to the unit-step input. Selecting the Find N(s)/D(s) option from the svstuff options, the closed-loop transfer function of the system with state feedback is

$$\frac{Y(s)}{R(s)} = \frac{1}{s^3 + 3s^2 + 7s + 5} \tag{10-44}$$

We can easily show by applying the final-value theorem to Equation 10-43 that the final value of $y(t)$ to a unit-step input is 1/5. Thus, while the state-feedback design places the eigenvalues at desired values, it does not, and often does not, guarantee the steady-state performance. In fact, state-feedback control with constant-gain feedback is generally useful only for regulator systems for which the system is not required to track inputs.

10.6.1 State Feedback with Integral Control

In general, there is a large class of control systems that must track inputs. One solution to this problem is to introduce an integral control, just as with the PI controller, together with the constant-gain state feedback. The block diagram of a system with constant-gain state feedback and integral control feedback of the output is shown in Figure 10-18. For an SISO system, the integral control adds one integrator to the system. As shown in Figure 10-18, the output of the $(n + 1)st$ integrator is designated as x_{n+1}. The system equations are written from Figure 10-18.

$$\frac{d\mathbf{x}(t)}{dt} = \mathbf{Ax}(t) + \mathbf{B}u(t) \qquad (10\text{-}45)$$

where $\mathbf{x}(t)$ is the $n \times 1$ state vector, and $u(t)$ is the scalar input.

$$u(t) = -\mathbf{Kx}(t) + Gx_{n-1}(t) \qquad (10\text{-}46)$$

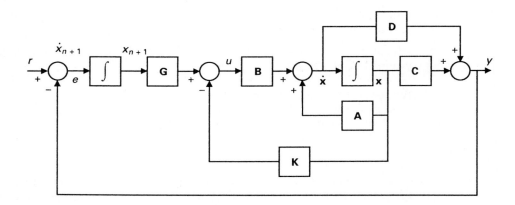

Figure 10-18. Block diagram of control system with state feedback and integral-output feedback.

where $\mathbf{K}$ is the state-feedback matrix given by Equation 10-33, and G is the scalar integral-feedback gain.

$$y(t) = \mathbf{Cx}(t) + Du(t)$$
$$= (\mathbf{C} - \mathbf{DK})\mathbf{x}(t) + DGx_{n+1}(t) \qquad (10\text{-}47)$$

$$\frac{dx_{n+1}(t)}{dt} = e(t) = r(t) - y(t) \qquad (10\text{-}48)$$

Substituting Equation 10-46 into Equation 10-45, and Equation 10-47 into Equation 10-48, the $n + 1$ state equations of the closed-loop system with integral output feedback are written in vector-matrix form.

$$\begin{bmatrix} \dfrac{d\mathbf{x}(t)}{dt} \\[2ex] \dfrac{dx_{n+1}(t)}{dt} \end{bmatrix} = \begin{bmatrix} \mathbf{A} - \mathbf{BK} & \mathbf{B}G \\ D\mathbf{K} - \mathbf{C} & -DG \end{bmatrix} \begin{bmatrix} \mathbf{x}(t) \\ x_{n+1}(t) \end{bmatrix} + \begin{bmatrix} 0 \\ 1 \end{bmatrix} r(t) \qquad (10\text{-}49)$$

Thus, the closed-loop system with state and integral-output feedback is described by the state equation:

$$\frac{d\overline{\mathbf{x}}(t)}{dt} = \overline{\mathbf{A}}\overline{\mathbf{x}}(t) + \overline{\mathbf{B}}r(t) \qquad (10\text{-}50)$$

where

$\overline{\mathbf{x}}(t)$ is the composite $n + 1$-dimensional state vector, and

$$\overline{\mathbf{A}} = \begin{bmatrix} \mathbf{A} - \mathbf{BK} & \mathbf{B}G \\ D\mathbf{K} - \mathbf{C} & -DG \end{bmatrix} \qquad \overline{\mathbf{B}} = \begin{bmatrix} 0 \\ 1 \end{bmatrix} \qquad (10\text{-}51)$$

The design is carried out by assigning eigenvalues to the closed-loop system, and matching the characteristic equation $|\lambda\mathbf{I} - \overline{\mathbf{A}}|$ to that with the desired eigenvalues.

The function svstuff can be used to carry the design of state feedback with integral-output control under the "State-feedback" option. Let us use the same system described in Equation 10-42 as an illustrative example.

After entering the transfer function of Equation 10-42 in svstuff, representing the system in CCF, and selecting State feedback, the following dialog and results are obtained:

```
Include Integral Control of output? [n] > y <CR>
Enter vector of 4 desired pole locations > [-1 -2 -1+2*i -1-2*i] <CR>
State feedback with integral control is:
      u = -Kx +G*integral(r - y)
  K =
     19    13    4
  G = 10
```

The unit-step response of the closed-loop system is shown in Figure 10-19. Notice that the final value of $y(t)$ is now unity. It is easy to see from Figure 10-18 that the open-loop transfer function of the system with integral feedback control is simply the closed-loop transfer function of the system with only state feedback in Equation 10-37 multiplied by G/s. Thus,

$$\frac{Y(s)}{E(s)} = \frac{10}{s(s^3 + 3s^2 + 7s + 5)} \qquad (10\text{-}52)$$

which is a type 1 system.

As an alternative, the desired poles may be entered as > roots([c])

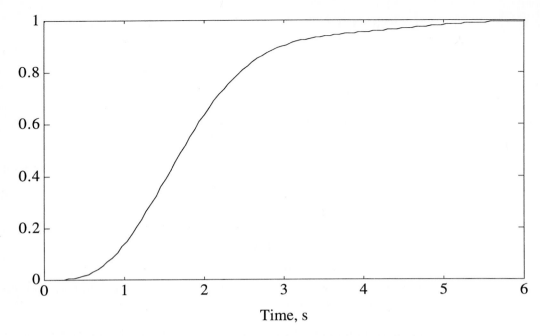

Time, s

Figure 10-19. Unit-step response of a system with process described by Equation 10-42 with state-feedback and integral-output-feedback control.

`<CR>`, where `c` represents the coefficients of the characteristic polynomial with the desired poles.

EXERCISES

Unless otherwise stated, the systems in the following problems all have a unity-feedback configuration for the closed-loop system.

10-1. The plant transfer function $G_p(s)$ and the transfer function of the series PI controller are given as

$$G_p(s) = \frac{100}{s^2 + 10s + 100} \qquad G_c(s) = K_p + \frac{K_i}{s}$$

(a) Find the value of K_i so that the ramp-error constant K_v is 100.

(b) With the value of K_i found in part a, plot the root loci of the characteristic equation for positive K_p. Find the critical value of K_p for the system to be stable. Use `tddesign`.

(c) Using the value of K_i found in part a, find the value of K_p when the maximum overshoot is near minimum. What is the value of this maximum overshoot? Use `tddesign`.

10-2. The Hubble space telescope is modeled as a second-order transfer function,

$$G_p(s) = \frac{0.00667}{s^2 + 0.00667}$$

The PID controller is used to improve the stability of the closed-loop system with unity feedback. The performance specifications are

Ramp-error constant $K_v = 100$
Rise time $t_r < 1$ s
Settling time $t_s < 3$ s
Maximum % overshoot < 5

Design the PID controller parameters, K_p, K_d, and K_i so that the performance specifications are satisfied.

10-3. The plant transfer function of an inventory control system is

$$G_c(s) = \frac{4}{s^2}$$

A series PD controller with $G_c(s) = K_p + K_d s$ is used to improve the performance of the system. Find the values of K_p and K_d so that the following performance specifications are satisfied:

Rise time $t_r < 0.05$ s
Settling time < 0.1 s
Maximum overshoot $< 2\%$

Use `tddesign`.

10-4. For the inventory control system given in Problem 10-3, the series controller is to be a phase-lead controller,

$$G_c(s) = \frac{1 + aTs}{1 + Ts} \qquad a > 1$$

Determine the values of a and T so that the following performance specifications are satisfied:

Rise time $t_r < 0.2$ s
Settling time $t_s < 0.5$ s
Maximum overshoot $< 5\%$

Use `tddesign`.

10-5. Carry out the design of the system in Problem 10-1 using the frequency domain method and `fddesign`.

10-6. Carry out the design of the system in Problem 10-2 using the frequency domain method and `fddesign`.

10-7. Carry out the design of the system in Problem 10-3 using the frequency domain method and `fddesign`.

10-8. Carry out the design of the system in Problem 10-4 using the frequency domain method and `fddesign`.

Exercises   **163**

10-9. The transfer function of the process of a unity-feedback control system is

$$G_p(s) = \frac{60}{s(1 + 0.2s)(1 + 0.5s)}$$

Design a phase-lag controller so that the phase margin of the system is greater than 60°. Determine the values of M_p, gain margin, and BW of the compensated system. Compute and plot the unit-step response of the compensated system. Use fddesign.

10.10. The process transfer function of a steel-rolling system is given as

$$G_p(s) = \frac{5e^{-0.1s}}{s(1 + 0.1s)(1 + 0.5s)}$$

Design a series controller (phase lead or phase lag) so that the following performance specifications are satisfied:

      Rise time $t_r < 2$ s
      Maximum overshoot $< 5\%$

   (a) Use the time-domain design with tddesign.
   (b) Use the frequency-domain design with fddesign.

10-11. For the process described in Equation 10-42, represent the process in OCF, and carry out the state-feedback design for the closed-loop system to have eigenvalues at -1, $-1 + j1$, and $-1 - j1$.

10-12. Repeat Problem 10-11 with integral-output and state feedback. In addition to the three eigenvalues specified, the fourth one is to be at -10.

10-13. For the process described in Problem 10-10, approximate the time delay by tfde-lay(0.1,1). Design the closed-loop system with state and integral feedback with the desired eigenvalues at -10, -10, -100, $-10 + j10$, and $-10 - j10$. Find the feedback matrix **K** and the integral feedback gain G. Plot the unit-step response of the designed system.

Part

3

CSAD Toolbox Reference

Reference

This section of the text contains detailed descriptions of the major function M-files in the *CSAD Toolbox*. It begins with a list of all functions grouped by subject then continues with reference entries in alphabetical order. All *CSAD Toolbox* functions are listed subsequently, but only those intended for direct use have reference entries. The remainder are utilities called by the major toolbox functions.

Just as MATLAB offers on-line help, the functions in the *CSAD Toolbox* also provide on-line help by typing: >>help function where function is the name of a function in the *CSAD Toolbox*. In addition typing: >>help csad gives a brief listing of the most useful functions in the toolbox.

Interactive Plotting	
bplot	Bode plot
iltplot	inverse Laplace transform plot
mvpplot	magnitude versus phase frequency domain plot
plrplot	polar frequency domain plot
rlplot	root-locus plot
svplot	step response plot given state-variable description
tftplot	step response plot given transfer function description

Control System Analysis and Design	
`fddesign`	frequency domain design
`routh`	Routh-Hurwitz analysis
`svstuff`	state-variable analysis and design
`tddesign`	time-domain design

Transfer Function Manipulation	
`pfe`	partial-fraction expansion
`tf2ccf`	convert to controllable canonical form
`tf2ocf`	convert to observable canonical form
`tfcancel`	perform pole-zero cancelation
`tfcloop`	find closed-loop transfer function
`tfdelay`	find transfer function of a pure delay
`tfderiv`	find derivative of a transfer function
`tfmonic`	make denominator monic
`tford2`	find second-order transfer function
`tfparall`	find transfer function of parallel connection
`tfseries`	find transfer function of series connection

State-Variable Manipulation	
`cmatrix`	controllability matrix
`omatrix`	observability matrix
`sv2sv`	state-variable transformation
`sv2tf`	convert to transfer function
`svcloop`	find closed-loop state variables
`svparall`	find state variables of parallel connection
`svseries`	find state variables of series connection
`tr2ccf`	find transformation to controllable canonical form
`tr2df`	find transformation to diagonal form
`tr2ocf`	find transformation to observable canonical form

Polynomial Manipulation	
`padd`	addition
`pmake`	construct polynomial from roots
`pmult`	multiplication
`pderiv`	differentiation
`psim`	eliminate leading zero coefficients

Control System Utilities	
fdspecs	find frequency domain specifications
invlt	compute inverse Laplace transform
marstab	find marginal stability point
nichmag	compute Nichols magnitude curves
stepsize	find step size for time-domain plots
svstep	compute step response
td2fd	find frequency domain specifications from time-domain specifications
tdspecs	find time-domain specifications
tfess	find error constants and steady-state error
tfresp	compute frequency response
tfstep	compute step response

Input/Output Utilities	
displist	display annotated list
ninput	single-number prompt
pinput	polynomial prompt
pzshow	pole-zero display
svshow	display state variable matrices
tfshow	display transfer function
vinput	vector prompt
yninput	yes/no prompt

General Utilities	
between	limit variable range
ccp	form complex conjugate pair
db2r	convert from decibels to ratio
fixaxis	fix plot axes from user prompt
linterp	linear interpolation
p2str	polynomial to string conversion
p2r	polar to rectangular conversion
plotutil	utilities for plotting functions
r2db	convert from ratio to dB
r2p	rectangular to polar conversion
tolower	change to lowercase

Purpose

Interactive plotting of Bode frequency response plots.

Synopsis

```
bplot
bplot(N,D)
bplot(N,D,k1,k2)
```

Description

bplot computes and plots the magnitude and phase frequency response of continuous-time linear time-invariant systems given their transfer function description.

bplot prompts the user for the numerator and denominator polynomials, N and D, respectively. It also prompts the user for the frequency range by asking for k1 and k2 where $10^{k1} < w < 10^{k2}$ is the range in radians per second.

bplot(N,D) uses N and D as the numerator and denominator polynomials, respectively, and prompts the user for the frequency range.

bplot(N,D,k1,k2) in addition uses k1 and k2 as the frequency range.

The user interacts with bplot by entering the *first letter* of the option desired when the following list is presented:

```
                    - BODEPLOT OPTIONS -

            Amplitude    Freq range
            Phase        Time delay
            Both         New TF
            Zoom in      Change O/C
            Set axes     Display TF
            Grid         Margins
            Hold         Roots
            Label        View Data
                         Quit
```

The first letter is entered and the return key is pressed. The action taken by each option is described as follows:

a   The amplitude or magnitude plot is generated given the current N,D,k1,k2.

p   The phase plot is generated given the current N,D,k1,k2.

b   Both the amplitude and phase plot are shown simultaneously.

z   The user is asked to chose an area of the plot to enlarge by using the mouse. Plot grid and titles are lost.

s   The user is prompted for numerical values for the axis limits. The default response is to keep the present value.

g   A grid is drawn on the current plot. Does not work when Both is selected.

h   Toggles the current state of hold. When hold is on, the future plots are plotted on top of the current plot. When off, future plots appear on a new plotting surface.

l   Prompts the user for a title to place on the plot.

f   Prompts the user for a new frequency range to plot.

t   Prompts the user for the time delay in seconds associated with the current transfer function.

n   Prompts the user for a new transfer function. Default entry is to keep the current transfer function.

c   Changes the transfer function to or from an open or closed loop unity feedback transfer function.

d   Displays the current transfer function, and shows the current time delay.

m   Computes the gain and phase margins, and associated crossover frequencies for the current transfer function.

r   Displays the zeros and poles of the current transfer function.

v   Prompts the user to identify a point on the current graph where the actual data is desired. The frequency, amplitude, and phase of 15 points near the chosen point are displayed numerically.

q   Quits the function and returns control to the calling function or command screen.

There are six options not shown that also may be entered. They are

' '   (A space and/or a return key). Show the current graph.

@   Prompts the user for text, then places the text at a point on the current graph as instructed by the user.

Gets the coordinates of the graph pointed to by the user.

–   Prompts the user for the endpoints of a line, then plots a dotted line on the current graph.

^   Allows the user to set some of the parameters used within the function.

!   Passes the rest of the line entered to the function for evaluation and execution. All text following the exclamation point is evaluated. This command allows access to the internal variables of the function and allows the user to issue any MATLAB command. For example, !meta creates a graphics metafile of the current plot.

Algorithm

bplot is an M-file in the *CSAD Toolbox*. It uses only standard MATLAB commands and other functions in the *CSAS Toolbox*. As with most numerical procedures, the accuracy of this function may deteriorate under several conditions. Keeping the order of the transfer function small (i.e., <10) and not letting any system poles appear on the imaginary axis is helpful.

See also

mvpplot, plrplot

Purpose

To form a complex conjugate pair given real and imaginary parts.

Synopsis

```
ccp(real,imag)
```

Description

`ccp(real,imag)` returns two complex numbers, `real+j*imag` and `real−j*imag` as a column vector.

`ccp` is useful for composing polynomials using `poly`. For example,

$$\text{poly}([0;-1+j*2;-1-j*2]) = \text{poly}([0;\text{ccp}(-1,2)])$$

$$= s^3 + 2s^2 + 5s$$

Algorithm

`ccp` is an M-file in the *CSAD Toolbox*. Only standard MATLAB commands are used.

Purpose

To construct the controllability matrix associated with the system written in state variable form as

$$\frac{d\mathbf{x}}{dt} = \mathbf{A}\mathbf{x} + \mathbf{B}u, \, y = \mathbf{C}\mathbf{x} + Du$$

Synopsis

```
cmatrix(A,B)
```

Description

`cmatrix(A,B)` finds the controllability matrix

$$[\mathbf{B} \ \mathbf{AB} \ \mathbf{A}^2\mathbf{B} \cdots \mathbf{A}^{n-1}\mathbf{B}].$$

If the rank of the controllability matrix is equal to n, the order of the system, the system is said to be controllable.

Algorithm

`cmatrix` is an M-file in the *CSAD Toolbox*. Only standard MATLAB commands are used.

See also

```
omatrix, svstuff
```

Purpose

To interactively design lead and lag type cascade controllers from frequency domain specifications.

Synopsis

```
fddesign
fddesign(N,D)
```

Description

fddesign prompts the user for the numerator and denominator polynomials of the plant to be controlled. Then, values for the controller parameters are requested.

fddesign(N,D) starts with N and D as the numerator and denominator polynomials of the plant to be controlled.

The lead and lag controllers have a transfer function

$$G_c(s) = K\frac{1 + aTs}{1 + Ts} \qquad \begin{array}{l} a > 1 = \text{lead} \\[4pt] a < 1 = \text{lag} \end{array}$$

where K is the DC gain, and T and a are parameters. a is greater than 1 for lead compensation and less than 1 for lag compensation.

The user interacts with tddesign by entering the *first letter* of the option desired when the following list is presented:

```
                     – FDDESIGN OPTIONS –
          Controller values      Step Response
          Frequency Response     Display TF's
          Lead/Lag math          Poles and Zeros
          Goals to meet          New Plant TF
          Error, steady state    Quit
```

The first letter is entered and the return key is pressed. The action taken by each option is described as follows:

c   The user is prompted for new controller values. The default input is to keep the current values.

f   Calls the CSAD function bplot to find the frequency response. The user can choose to find the response of the plant multiplied by K, the controller, the open-loop system, or the closed loop system. See command ^ below for changing the plot type.

l   For lead controllers, calculates the required parameter a that gives a specified peak phase in degrees. For lag controllers, calculates the required parameter a that gives a specified attenuation in dB.

g   Prompts the user for the maximum allowable percent overshoot, the minimum rise time, and the minimum settling time. Based on the standard second order transfer function, the user is supplied with a minimum-phase margin, maximum-peak resonance, and minimum-closed-loop bandwidth for the dominant poles of the closed-loop system.

e   Calculates the steady-state error of the system to both a unit step and unit ramp input. This information provides assistance in setting K.

s   Calls the CSAD function `tftplot` to plot the step response of the system. The user can choose among the variables e, u, and y to plot where e is the error variable $y - r$, u is the output of the controller and plant input, and y is the system output.

d   Displays the plant, controller, and closed-loop system transfer functions.

p   Displays the poles and zeros of the plant, controller, and closed-loop transfer functions.

n   Prompts the user for a new plant transfer function.

q   Quits the function and returns control to the calling function or command screen.

There are four options not shown that also may be entered. They are

^   Allows one to change the type of frequency response plot. The default is `bplot`. Choices are: `bplot`, `mvplot`, `plrplot`.

h   Toggles the current state of hold. When hold is on, the future plots are plotted on top of the current plot. When off, future plots appear on a new plotting surface. This command is useful for comparing new step response plots with prior designs. Both `rlplot` and `tftplot` turn hold off when they are terminated.

' '   (A space or a return key). Shows the current graph.

!   Passes the rest of the line entered to the function for evaluation and execution. All text following the exclamation point is evaluated. This command allows access to the internal variables of the function and allows the user to issue any MATLAB command. For example, `!meta` creates a graphics metafile of the current plot.

Algorithm

fddesign is an M-file in the *CSAD Toolbox*. It uses only standard MATLAB commands and other functions in the *CSAD Toolbox*. As with most numerical procedures, the accuracy of this function may deteriorate under a number of conditions. Keeping the order of the transfer function small (i.e., <10) is helpful.

See also

bplot, mvpplot, plrplot, tftplot, tddesign

Purpose

To plot the time response of a function given its Laplace transform.

Synopsis

```
iltplot
iltplot(N,D)
```

Description

iltplot computes and plots the inverse Laplace transform of continuous-time functions that can be represented by rational polynomials.

iltplot prompts the user for the numerator and denominator polynomials, N and D, respectively, of the given function.

iltplot(N,D) uses N and D as the numerator and denominator polynomials, respectively.

The user interacts with iltplot by entering the *first letter* of the option desired when the following list is presented:

```
                    - ILTPLOT OPTIONS -

            Plot          Final time
            Zoom in       New N,D
            Set axes      Display
            Grid plot     Roots
            Hold plot     View data
            Label Plot    Quit
```

The first letter is entered and the return key is pressed. The action taken by each option is described as follows:

p   A plot of the time response is generated given the current N,D.
z   The user is asked to choose an area of the plot to enlarge by using the mouse. Plot grid and titles are lost.
s   The user is prompted for numerical values for the axis limits. The default response is to keep the present value.
g   A grid is drawn on the current plot.
h   Toggles the current state of hold. When hold is on, the future plots are plotted on top of the current plot. When off, future plots appear on a new plotting surface.

l Prompts the user for a title and *y*-axis label to place on the plot.

f Prompts the user for a new final computation time.

n Prompts the user for a new transfer function. Default entry is to keep the current transfer function.

d Displays the current transfer function.

r Displays the zeros and poles of the current transfer function.

v Prompts the user to identify a point on the current graph where the actual data is desired. The response and associated time of 15 points near the chosen point are displayed numerically.

q Quits the function and returns control to the calling function or command screen.

There are six options not shown that also may be entered. They are

' ' (A space or a return key). Show the current graph.

@ Prompts the user for text then places the text at a point on the current graph as instructed by the user.

Gets the coordinates of the graph pointed to by the user.

– Prompts the user for the endpoints of a line, then plots a dotted line on the current graph.

^ Allows the user to set some of the parameters used within the function.

! Passes the rest of the line entered to the function for evaluation and execution. All text following the exclamation point is evaluated. This command allows access to the internal variables of the function and allows the user to issue any MATLAB command. For example, !meta creates a graphics metafile of the current plot.

Algorithm

iltplot is an M-file in the *CSAD Toolbox*. It uses only standard MATLAB commands and other functions in the *CSAD Toolbox*. As with most numerical procedures, the accuracy of this function may deteriorate under several conditions. Keeping the order of the function small (i.e., <10) is helpful.

See also tftplot

Purpose

Interactive plotting of frequency-response plots in magnitude-versus-phase format.

Synopsis

```
mvpplot
mvpplot(N,D)
mvpplot(N,D,k1,k2)
```

Description

mvpplot computes and plots the magnitude versus phase frequency response of continuous-time LTI systems given their transfer function description.

mvpplot prompts the user for the numerator and denominator polynomials, N and D, respectively. It also prompts the user for the frequency range by asking for k1 and k2 where $10^{k1} < w < 10^{k2}$ is the range in radians per second.

mvpplot(N,D) uses N and D as the numerator and denominator polynomials, respectively, and prompts the user for the frequency range.

mvpplot(N,D,k1,k2) in addition uses k1 and k2 as the frequency range.

The user interacts with mvpplot by entering the first letter of the option desired when the following list is presented:

```
                        – MVPPLOT OPTIONS –

            Plot              Freq range
            Zoom in           Time delay
            Set axes          New TF
            Grid              Change O/C
            Hold              Display TF
            Add Nichols       Margins
            Label plot        Roots
            w on plot         View data
                              Quit
```

The *first letter* is entered and the return key is pressed. The action taken by each option is described as follows:

p   The magnitude versus phase plot is generated given the current N,D,k1,k2.

z   The user is asked to choose an area of the plot to enlarge by using a mouse. Plot grid, Nichols grid, and titles are lost.

s   The user is prompted for numerical values for the axis limits. The default response is to keep the present value.

g   A grid is drawn on the current plot

h   Toggles the current state of hold. When hold is on, the future plots are plotted on top of the current plot. When off, future plots appear on a new plotting surface.

a   Plots Nichols constant closed-loop magnitude grid lines on the current plot. 9-, 6-, 3-, 1-, 0-, −1-, −3-, −6-, and −9-dB grids are added. The −3-dB grid is dash-dotted, and the others are dotted.

l   Prompts the user for a title to place on the plot.

w   Prompts the user to identify a point on the current plot. The value of ω at the selected point is returned and optionally labeled on the plot.

f   Prompts the user for a new frequency range to plot.

t   Prompts the user for the time delay in seconds associated with the current transfer function.

n   Prompts the user for a new transfer function. Default entry is to keep the current transfer function.

c   Change the current transfer function to or from an open or closed loop unity feedback transfer function.

d   Displays the current transfer function, and shows the current time delay.

m   Computes the gain and phase margins, and associated crossover frequencies for the current transfer function.

r   Displays the zeros and poles of the current transfer function.

v   Prompts the user to identify a point on the current graph where the actual data is desired. The frequency, amplitude, and phase of 15 points near the chosen point are displayed numerically.

q   Quits the function and returns control to the calling function or command screen.

There are six options not shown that also may be entered. They are

' '   (A space or a return key). Shows the current graph.

@   Prompts the user for text then places the text at a point on the current graph as instructed by the user.

\#   Gets the coordinates of the graph pointed to by the user.

−   Prompts the user for the endpoints of a line, then plots a dotted line on the current graph.

^   Allows the user to set some of the parameters used within the function.

!   Passes the rest of the line entered to the function for evaluation and execution. All text following the exclamation point is evaluated. This command allows access to the internal variables of the function and allows the user to issue any MATLAB command. For example, !meta creates a graphics metafile of the current plot.

Algorithm

mvpplot is an M-file in the *CSAD Toolbox*. It uses only standard MATLAB commands and other functions in the *CSAD Toolbox*. As with most numerical procedures, the accuracy of this function may deteriorate under a number of conditions. Keeping the order of the transfer function small (i.e., <10) and not letting any system poles appear on the imaginary axis is helpful.

See also

bplot, plrplot

Purpose

To construct the observability matrix associated with the system written in state variable form as

$$\frac{d\mathbf{x}}{dt} = \mathbf{A}\mathbf{x} + \mathbf{B}u, \, y = \mathbf{C}\mathbf{x} + Du$$

Synopsis

```
omatrix(A,C)
```

Description

`omatrix(A,C)` finds the observability matrix

$$\begin{bmatrix} \mathbf{C} \\ \mathbf{CA} \\ \mathbf{CA}^2 \\ \vdots \\ \mathbf{CA}^{n-1} \end{bmatrix}$$

If the rank of the observability matrix is equal to n, the order of the system, the system is said to be observable.

Algorithm

`omatrix` is an M-file in the *CSAD Toolbox*. Only standard MATLAB commands are used.

See also

```
cmatrix, svstuff
```

Purpose

Polynomial addition.

Synopsis

```
padd(p0,p1,···,p9)
```

Description

padd adds up to 10 polynomial vectors.

Example

If $A(s) = 10s^3 + 2s^2 + 5s + 20$, $B(s) = s + 7$, and $C(s) = s^2 + 4s + 12$, then the sum $A(s) + B(s) + C(s) = 10s^3 + 3s^2 + 10s + 39$ can be found by entering

```
>>a = [10  2  5  20]
a =
      10  2  5  20
>>b = [1  7]
b =
      1   7
>>c = [1  4  12]
c =
      1  4  12
>>padd(a,b,c)
ans =
      10  3  10  39
```

Algorithm

padd is an M-file in the *CSAD Toolbox*. It uses only standard MATLAB commands.

See also

```
pmult
```

Purpose

To assist in finding the inverse Laplace transform through partial fraction expansion.

Synopsis

```
pfe
pfe(N,D)
```

Description

pfe computes the partial fraction expansion of $N(s)/D(s)$ after prompting the user for $N(s)$ and $D(s)$.

pfe(N,D) uses N and D as the numerator and denominator polynomials, respectively.

In addition to showing the individual terms in the partial fraction expansion, the corresponding time domain function is also shown.

Limitation

pfe cannot handle real poles of multiplicity greater than 2 and complex poles of multiplicity greater than 1. To get around this limitation, use the standard MATLAB function residue.

Algorithm

pfe is an M-file in the *CSAD Toolbox*. It uses only standard MATLAB commands. residue is called to find the poles and partial fraction expansion constants (i.e., the residues). As with most numerical procedures, the accuracy of this function may deteriorate under a several conditions. Keeping the order of the function small (i.e., <10) is helpful.

See also

```
iltplot, tftplot, padd, pmult
```

Purpose

Interactive plotting of frequency response plots in polar format.

Synopsis

```
plrplot
plrplot(N,D)
plrplot(N,D,k1,k2)
```

Description

plrplot computes and plots the polar (imaginary versus real part) frequency response of continuous-time LTI systems given their transfer function description.

plrplot prompts the user for the numerator and denominator polynomials, N and D, respectively. It also prompts the user for the frequency range by asking for k1 and k2 where $10^{k1} < w < 10^{k2}$ is the range in radians per second.

plrplot(N,D) uses N and D as the numerator and denominator polynomials, respectively, and prompts the user for the frequency range.

plrplot(N,D,k1,k2) in addition uses k1 and k2 as the frequency range.

The user interacts with plrplot by entering the *first letter* of the option desired when the following list is presented:

```
                    - PLRPLOT OPTIONS -
          Plot          Freq range
          Zoom in       Time delay
          Set axes      New TF
          Grid          Change O/C
          Hold          Display TF
          Label plot    Margins
          w on plot     Roots
          View data     Quit
```

The *first letter* is entered, and the return key is pressed. The action taken by each option is described as follows:

p   The polar plot is generated given the current N,D,k1,k2. The unit circle is also displayed dotted.

z The user is asked to choose an area of the plot to enlarge by using the mouse. Plot grid and labels are lost.

s The user is prompted for numerical values for the axis limits. The default response is to keep the present value.

g A grid is drawn on the current plot.

h Toggles the current state of hold. When hold is on, the future plots are plotted on top of the current plot. When off, future plots appear on a new plotting surface.

u Plots a unit circle grid on the current plot.

l Prompts the user for a title to place on the plot.

w Prompts the user to identify a point on the current plot. The value of ω at the selected point is returned and optionally labeled on the plot.

f Prompts the user for a new frequency range to plot.

t Prompts the user for the time delay in seconds associated with the current transfer function.

n Prompts the user for a new transfer function. Default entry is to keep the current transfer function.

c Changes the current transfer function to or from an open or closed loop unity feedback transfer function.

d Displays the current transfer function and shows the current time delay.

m Computes the gain and phase margins and associated crossover frequencies for the current transfer function.

r Displays the zeros and poles of the current transfer function.

v Prompts the user to identify a point on the current graph where the actual data is desired. The frequency, amplitude, and phase of 15 points near the chosen point are displayed numerically.

q Quits the function and returns control to the calling function or command screen.

There are six options not shown that also may be entered. They are

' ' (A space or a return key). Show the current graph.

@ Prompts the user for text then places the text at a point on the current graph as instructed by the user.

Gets the coordinates of the graph pointed to by the user.

− Prompts the user for the endpoints of a line, then plots a dotted line on the current graph.

^ Allows the user to set some of the parameters used within the function.

! Passes the rest of the line entered to the function for evaluation and execution. All text following the exclamation point is evaluated. This command allows access to the internal variables of the function and allows the user to issue any MATLAB command. For example, !meta creates a graphics metafile of the current plot.

Algorithm

plrplot is an M-file in the *CSAD Toolbox*. It uses only standard MATLAB commands and other functions in the *CSAD Toolbox*. As with most numerical procedures, the accuracy of this function may deteriorate under a number of conditions. Keeping the order of the transfer function small (i.e., <10) and not letting any system poles appear on the imaginary axis is helpful.

See also

bplot, mvpplot

Purpose

To construct polynomials from a list of its roots.

Synopsis

```
pmake(r0,r1, . . . ,r9)
```

Description

`pmake` constructs real polynomials from a list of root locations. This function acts like `poly`, but offers more flexible input. `pmake` features:

1. Root locations can be entered as separate input arguments, for example,

```
pmake(-1,-2,-3) = poly([-1;-2;-3])
```

2. Each input argument can be a vector of roots, for example,

```
pmake([-1,-2,-3,-4]) = pmake([-1;-2;-3;-4])
```

3. The output is always a strictly *real* polynomial. Complex conjugate roots are added if they do not appear in the input, for example,

```
pmake(-1+sqrt(-1)*2) =
poly([-1+sqrt(-1)*2;-1-sqrt(-1)*2]).
```

Algorithm

`pmake` is an M-file in the *CSAD Toolbox*. It uses only standard MATLAB commands.

See also

```
poly, ccp
```

Purpose

Polynomial multiplication.

Synopsis

```
pmult(p0,p1, . . . ,p9)
```

Description

pmult adds up to 10 polynomial vectors.

Example

If $A(s) = 10s^3 + 2s^2 + 5s + 20$, $B(s) = s + 7$, and $C(s) = s^2 + 4s + 12$, then the product $A(s)\cdot B(s)\cdot C(s) = 10s^6 + 112s^5 + 427s^4 + 995s^3 + 588s^2 + 1220s + 1680$ can be found by entering:

```
>>a = [10 2 5 20]
a =
      10    2    5    20
>>b = [1 7]
b =
      1    7
>>c = [1 4 12]
c =
      1    4    12
>>pmult(a,b,c)
ans =
   Columns 1 through 6
        10      112     427      995      588     1220
   Column 7
        1680
```

Algorithm

pmult is an M-file in the *CSAD Toolbox*. It uses the standard MATLAB command conv.

See also

```
padd, conv
```

Purpose

To plot the root locus of a system.

Synopsis

```
rlplot
rlplot(N,D)
```

Description

rlplot computes and plots the root locus of continuous-time systems given their characteristic equation of the form: $1 + K*N(s)/D(s) = 0$.

rlplot prompts the user for the numerator and denominator polynomials, N and D, respectively, of the desired characteristic equation.

rlplot(N,D) uses N and D as the numerator and denominator polynomials, respectively.

The user interacts with rlplot by entering the *first letter* of the option desired when the following list is presented:

– RLPLOT OPTIONS –

K values	Zeta line
Single K	Wn circle
Find K	Rule info
Marginal K	New/clear
Grid	Display TF
Title	Quit

The *first letter* is entered, and the return key is pressed. The action taken by each option is described as follows:

k   Prompts the user for values of *K* where the root locus is desired and plots the resulting locus. Any MATLAB vector statement is valid as input. For example, entering logspace(-1,3,50) computes the root locus for 50 logarithmically spaced points starting at 10^{-1} and ending at 10^3. Or, entering linspace(0,20) computes the root locus at 100 linearly spaced points starting at 0 and ending at 20. Or, entering 10:5:100 computes the root locus starting at 10, ending at 100, with a linear increment of 5. Or, entering [-20 -10 -2 -6 10 25 -34] computes the root locus at the individually specified values given.

s   Finds and displays the roots of the characteristic equation for a single value of k but does not plot the result.

f   Prompts the user to identify a point on the root locus plot where the magnitude of K is desired. All the roots for this value of K are optionally marked on the graph.

m   Finds a value of K where the root locus crosses the $j\omega$ axis.

g   A grid is drawn on the current plot.

t   Prompts the user for a title to place on the plot.

z   Prompts the user for a damping ratio value (ζ) and plots the lines of constant damping ratio on the current plot.

w   Prompts the user for an undamped natural frequency, and plots the circle of constant frequency on the current plot.

r   Displays all root locus construction information.

n   Prompts the user for a new transfer function. Default entry is to keep the current transfer function. In addition, the option of clearing the current plot is given.

d   Displays the current transfer function.

q   Quits the function and returns control to the calling function or command screen.

There are six options not shown that also may be entered. They are

' '   (A space or a return key). Shows the current graph.

@   Prompts the user for text then places the text at a point on the current graph as instructed by the user.

Gets the coordinates of the graph pointed to by the user.

–   Prompts the user for the endpoints of a line, then plots a dotted line on the current graph.

^   Allows the user to set some of the parameters used within the function.

!   Passes the rest of the line entered to the function for evaluation and execution. All text following the exclamation point is evaluated. This command allows access to the internal variables of the function and allows the user to issue any MATLAB command. For example, `!meta` creates a graphics metafile of the current plot.

Algorithm

`rlplot` is an M-file in the *CSAD Toolbox*. It uses only standard MATLAB commands and other functions in the *CSAD Toolbox*. As with most numerical procedures, the accuracy of this function may deteriorate under a number of conditions. Keeping the order of the transfer function small (i.e., <10) is helpful.

See also

      `tddesign`

Warning

You may obtain erroneous results on `Find K`, `Marginal K`, and `Rule info` if the leading coefficient of the numerator polynomial or the denominator polynomial is not unity.

Purpose

Routh array construction

Synopsis

```
routh
routh(D)
```

Description

`routh(D)` visually constructs and displays the Routh array of the polynomial given by D.

If D is not given, the user is prompted.

Zero rows are replaced with the auxiliary equation. Zero elements in the first column are replaced with $1e-5$.

See also

```
roots, poly
```

Purpose

State transformation.

Synopsis

[Abar,Bbar,Cbar,Dbar] = sv2sv(A,B,C,D,T)

Description

sv2sv performs the state transformation:

$$\mathbf{Abar = T^{-1}AT, \ Bbar = T^{-1}B, \ Cbar = CT, \ Dbar = D}$$

Algorithm

sv2sv is an M-file in the *CSAD Toolbox*. Only standard MATLAB commands are used.

See also

tr2ccf, tr2ocf, tr2df, svstuff

Purpose

Conversion from state variable representation to transfer function.

Synopsis

```
[N,D]=sv2tf(A,B,C)
[N,D]=sv2tf(A,B,C,D)
```

Description

sv2tf converts the SISO system described by the state variable matrices A,B,C,D into its transfer function description $N(s)/D(s)$ where N and D are the coefficients of $N(s)$ and $D(s)$, respectively. If D is zero, it can be omitted.

Algorithm

sv2tf is an M-file in the *CSAD Toolbox*. It uses standard MATLAB commands and other functions in the *CSAD Toolbox*.

See also

```
tf2ccf, tf2ocf, svstuff
```

Purpose

To find the composite state variable representation of two systems connected in a negative feedback loop.

Synopsis

```
[A,B,C,D]=svcloop(A1,B1,C1,D1,K)
[A,B,C,D]=svcloop(A1,B1,C1,D1,A2,B2,C2,D2)
```

Description

`svcloop(A1,B1,C1,D1,A2,B2,C2,D2)` finds the state variable representation of two SISO systems connected in negative feedback.

`A1,B1,C1,D1` are the state variable matrices of the system in the forward path and `A2,B2,C2,D2` are the matrices of the system in the feedback path.

`svcloop(A1,B1,C1,D1,K)` assumes that constant feedback equal to K is used. Thus, $K = 1$ gives unity feedback.

`A,B,C,D` is the state variable representation of the composite system. If `[A,B,C,D]` is not given the results are displayed.

Algorithm

`svcloop` is an M-file in the *CSAD Toolbox*. Only standard MATLAB commands are used.

See also

`svseries, svparall, tfcloop, tfseries, tfparall`

Purpose

Find the state variable description of a second order lowpass system given a desired damping ratio ζ, and an undamped natural frequency ω_n.

Synopsis

```
svord2
svord2(zeta,Wn)
[A,B,C,D]=svord2
[A,B,C,D]=svord2(zeta,Wn)
```

Description

`svord2` prompts the user for `zeta` and `Wn`, then computes the state variable matrices.

`svord2(zeta,Wn)` uses the given `zeta` and `Wn`.

If `[A,B,C,D]` is not given, the results are displayed.

Algorithm

`svord2` is an M-file in the *CSAD Toolbox*. Only standard MATLAB commands are used.

See also

```
tford2
```

Purpose

To find the composite state variable representation of two systems connected in parallel.

Synopsis

```
[A,B,C,D] = svparall(A1,B1,C1,D1,K)
[A,B,C,D] = svparall(A1,B1,C1,D1,A2,B2,C2,D2)
```

Description

svparall(A1,B1,C1,D1,A2,B2,C2,D2) finds the state variable representation of two SISO systems connected in parallel.

A1,B1,C1,D1 are the state variable matrices of one system and A2,B2,C2,D2 are the matrices of the other system.

svparall(A1,B1,C1,D1,K) assumes that System 2 is a constant gain equal to K.

A,B,C,D is the state variable representation of the composite system. If [A,B,C,D] is not given the results are displayed.

Algorithm

svparall is an M-file in the *CSAD Toolbox*. Only standard MATLAB commands are used.

See also

svseries, svcloop, tfcloop, tfseries, tfparall

Purpose

To plot the unit step response of a system given its state variable description.

Synopsis

```
svplot
svplot(A,B,C,D)
```

Description

svplot computes and plots the unit step response of continuous-time systems represented by state variables.

svplot prompts the user for the state variable matrices of the desired system.

svplot(A,B,C,D) uses A,B,C,D as the state variable matrices.

The user interacts with svplot by entering the *first letter* of the option desired when the following list is presented:

```
              - SVPLOT OPTIONS -
       Plot          Final time
       Zoom in        New A,B,C,D
       Set axes       Display sys
       Grid plot      Attributes
       Hold plot      Eigenvalues
       Label Plot     View data
                      Quit
```

The *first letter* is entered, and the return key is pressed. The action taken by each option is described as follows:

p   A plot of the unit step response is generated given the current N,D.
z   The user is asked to choose an area of the plot to enlarge by using a mouse or the keyboard.
s   The user is prompted for numerical values for the axis limits. The default response is to keep the present value.
g   A grid is drawn on the current plot.
h   Toggles the current state of hold. When hold is on, the future plots are plotted on top of the current plot. When off, future plots appear on a new plotting surface.
l   Prompts the user for a title and *y*-axis label to place on the plot.

f   Prompts the user for a new final computation time.

n   Prompts the user for new state variable matrices. Default entry is to keep current matrices.

d   Displays the current state variable matrices.

a   Computes and displays the attributes of the step response. The delay, rise, and settling times are computed as are the percent overshoot and time at the maximum.

e   Displays the eigenvalues of the current system.

v   Prompts the user to identify a point on the current graph where the actual data is desired. The response and associated time of 15 points near the chosen point are displayed numerically.

q   Quits the function and returns control to the calling function or command screen.

There are six options not shown that also may be entered. They are

' ' (A space and/or a return key). Shows the current graph.

@   Prompts the user for text then places the text at a point on the current graph as instructed by the user.

−   Prompts the user for the endpoints of a line, then plots a dotted line on the current graph.

Gets the coordinates of the graph pointed to by the user.

^   Allows the user to set some of the parameters used within the function.

!   Passes the rest of the line entered to the function for evaluation and execution. All text following the exclamation point is evaluated. This command allows access to the internal variables of the function and allows the user to issue any MATLAB command. For example, `!meta` creates a graphics metafile of the current plot.

Algorithm

`svplot` is an M-file in the *CSAD Toolbox*. It uses only standard MATLAB commands and other functions in the *CSAD Toolbox*. As with most numerical procedures, the accuracy of this function may deteriorate under a number of conditions. Keeping the order of the transfer function small (i.e., <10) is helpful.

See also

`tftplot, iltplot`

Purpose

To find the composite state variable representation of two systems connected in series (cascade).

Synopsis

```
[A,B,C,D] = svseries(A1,B1,C1,D1,K)
[A,B,C,D] = svseries(A1,B1,C1,D1,A2,B2,C2,D2)
```

Description

`svseries(A1,B1,C1,D1,A2,B2,C2,D2)` finds the state variable representation of two SISO systems connected in series.

`A1,B1,C1,D1` are the state variable matrices of the system providing input to the system described by the matrices `A2,B2,C2,D2`.

`svseries(A1,B1,C1,D1,K)` assumes that System 2 is a constant gain equal to K.

`A,B,C,D` is the state variable representation of the composite system. If `[A,B,C,D]` is not given the results are displayed.

Algorithm

`svseries` is an M-file in the *CSAD Toolbox*. Only standard MATLAB commands are used.

See also

`svparall, svcloop, tfcloop, tfseries, tfparall`

Purpose

Interactive state variable analysis and design.

Synopsis

```
svstuff
svstuff(A,B,C,D)
svstuff(N,D)
```

Description

svstuff is a menu driven function that performs a number of SISO state variable analysis tasks after prompting the user for state variable matrices.

svstuff(A,B,C,D) uses the state variable matrices A,B,C, and D. svstuff(N,D) converts the transfer function $N(s)/D(s)$ to state variable form, then offers the menu.

The user interacts with svstuff by entering the *first letter* of the option desired when the following list is presented:

```
              – SVSTUFF –

        Eigenvalues
        Controllability
        Observability
        Transformations
        State feedback
        Response to step
        Display A,B,C,D
        New A,B,C,D
        Find N(s)/D(s)
        Input N(s)/D(s)
        Quit
```

The *first letter* is entered, and the return key is pressed. The action taken by each option is described as follows:

e   The eigenvalues of the **A** matrix, that is, the system poles, are computed. If state feedback is used, the closed-loop eigenvalues are also displayed.

c   The controllability matrix is computed and its rank is found.

o   The observability matrix is computed and its rank is found.

t   State transformations to CCF, OCF, and DF are offered. CCF is controllable canonical form. OCF is observable canonical form, and DF is diagonal form. *Note*: CCF will fail if the system is not controllable, OCF will fail is the system is not observable, DF will fail is the system does not have distinct eigenvectors.

s   State feedback gains using Ackerman's formula are computed after the user is prompted for desired closed-loop pole locations. Note the system must be controllable. If the system is weakly controllable, the gains may become exceedingly large and the closed-loop poles may differ from those requested. Addition of integral control of the output is offered as an option.

r   The response to a unit step input is computed and plotted. The user is given the choice of finding the response with or without state feedback if state feedback gains are computed.

d   The state variable matrices are displayed.

n   The user is prompted for a new state variable representation for analysis. The default input is the current values.

f   The transfer function description is found with or without state feedback.

i   The user is prompted to input a transfer function, which is then converted to the state variable description in controllable or observable canonical form.

q   Quits the function and returns control to the calling function or command screen.

There is one option not shown that also may be entered. It is

!   Passes the rest of the line entered to the function for evaluation and execution. All text following the exclamation point is evaluated. This command allows access to the internal variables of the function and allows the user to issue any MATLAB command. For example, `!title('Step Response')` adds a title to the current plot.

Algorithm

`svstuff` is an M-file in the *CSAD Toolbox*. It uses only standard MATLAB commands and other functions in the *CSAD Toolbox*. As with most numerical procedures, the accuracy of this function may deteriorate under a number of conditions. Keeping the order of the system small (i.e., <10) is helpful.

See also

cmatrix, omatrix, sv2sv, sv2tf, tf2ccf, tf2ocf, tr2ccf, tr2ocf, tr2df

Purpose

To interactively design PID type cascade controllers from time domain specifications.

Synopsis

```
tddesign
tddesign(N,D)
```

Description

`tddesign` prompts the user for the numerator and denominator polynomials
of the plant to be controlled. Then, values for the PID parameters are requested.

`tddesign(N,D)` starts with `N` and `D` as the numerator and denominator polynomials of the plant to be controlled. Then values for the PID parameters are
requested.

The PID controller has a transfer function:

$$G_c(s) = K_p + K_d s + K_i/s$$

where K_p is the proportional gain, K_d is the derivative gain, and K_i is the integral
gain. P, PD, PI, and PID controllers can be considered by simply setting the
gains of undesired components to zero. For example, if K_p is nonzero and both
K_d and K_i are zero, a proportional controller is considered.

The user interacts with `tddesign` by entering the *first letter* of the option
desired when the following list is presented:

```
                    - TDDESIGN OPTIONS -

                    Controller values
                    Root locus
                    Step Response
                    Goals to meet
                    Error, steady state
                    Display TF's
                    Poles and Zeros
                    New Plant TF
                    Quit
```

The first letter is entered and the return key is pressed. The action taken by
each option is described as follows:

c   The user is prompted for new controller gains. The default input is to keep the current values.

r   Calls the CSAD function `rlplot` to perform root locus analysis. The user can choose K_p, K_d, or K_i as the root-locus variable. The remaining gains are set to their current values.

s   Calls the CSAD function `tftplot` to plot the step response of the system. The user can choose among the variables e, u, and y to plot where e is the error variable $y - r$, u is the output of the controller and plant input, and y is the system output.

g   Prompts the user for the maximum allowable percent overshoot, the minimum rise time, and the minimum settling time. Based on the standard second order transfer function, the user is supplied with a minimum damping ratio (ζ) and undamped natural frequency (ω_n) for the dominant poles of the closed loop system. This information is used for generating "ζ lines" and "ω_n circles" on root locus plots to assist in determining the optimum PID gain values.

e   Calculates the steady state error of the system to both a unit step and unit ramp input. This information provides assistance in setting K_p.

d   Displays the plant, controller, and closed-loop system transfer functions.

p   Displays the poles and zeros of the plant, controller, and closed-loop transfer functions.

n   Prompts the user for a new plant transfer function.

q   Quits the function and returns control to the calling function or command screen.

There are three options not shown that also may be entered. They are

h   Toggles the current state of hold. When hold is on, the future plots are plotted on top of the current plot. When off, future plots appear on a new plotting surface. This command is useful for comparing new step response plots with prior designs. Both `rlplot` and `tftplot` turn hold off when they are terminated.

' '   (A space or a return key). Shows the current graph.

!   Passes the rest of the line entered to the function for evaluation and execution. All text following the exclamation point is evaluated. This command allows access to the internal variables of the function and allows the user to issue any MATLAB command. For example, `!meta` creates a graphics metafile of the current plot.

Algorithm

`tddesign` is an M-file in the *CSAD Toolbox*. It uses only standard MATLAB commands and other functions in the *CSAD Toolbox*. As with most numerical procedures, the accuracy of this function may deteriorate under a number of conditions. Keeping the order of the transfer function small (i.e., <10) is helpful.

See also

```
tftplot, rlplot
```

Purpose

Convert a transfer function to a state variable representation in controllable canonical form (also known as phase variable canonical form).

Synopsis

```
[A,B,C,D]=tf2ccf(N,D)
```

Description

tf2ccf converts the transfer function having N and D as its numerator and denominator polynomials into controllable canonical form. In this form, the system is always controllable since the determinant of the controllability matrix is identically one.

Algorithm

tf2ccf is an M-file in the *CSAD Toolbox*. Only standard MATLAB commands are used.

See also

tf2ocf, sv2tf, tr2ccf, tr2ocf, tr2df, svstuff, sv2sv

Purpose

Convert a transfer function to a state variable representation in observable canonical form (also known as dual-phase variable canonical form).

Synopsis

    [A,B,C,D]=tf2ocf(N,D)

Description

tf2ocf converts the transfer function having N and D as its numerator and denominator polynomials into observable canonical form. In this form, the system is always observable because the determinant of the observability matrix is identically one.

Algorithm

tf2ocf is an M-file in the *CSAD Toolbox*. Only standard MATLAB commands are used.

See also

    tf2ccf, sv2tf, tr2ccf, tr2ocf, tr2df, svstuff, sv2sv

Purpose

To find the closed-loop transfer function given forward and feedback transfer functions.

Synopsis

```
[N,D] = tfcloop(Ng,Dg,K)
[N,D] = tfcloop(Ng,Dg,Nh,Dh)
```

Description

`tfcloop(Ng,Dg,Nh,Dh)` computes the closed-loop transfer function $M(s) = G(s)/[1 + G(s)H(s)]$ where `Ng` and `Dg` are the numerator and denominator of $G(s)$, and `Nh` and `Dh` are the numerator and denominator of $H(s)$.

`tfcloop(Ng,Dg,K)` assumes that $H(s) = K$. (Thus, $K = 1$ is unity feedback.)

`N` and `D` are the numerator and denominator of $M(s)$, respectively. If `N` and `D` are not given, the results are displayed.

Algorithm

`tfcloop` is an M-file in the *CSAD Toolbox*. It uses only standard MATLAB commands and other functions in the *CSAD Toolbox*.

See also

```
svparall, svcloop, svseries, tfseries, tfparall
```

Purpose

To find a rational transfer function approximation to a time delay.

Synopsis

```
[N,D] = tfdelay(T,M)
[N,D] = tfdelay(T,M,1)
```

Description

`tfdelay(T,M)` gives an *M*th-order *all-pass* transfer function approximation to a pure time delay of *T* seconds. N and D are the coefficients of the numerator and denominator polynomials respectively.

`tfdelay(T,M,1)` gives an *M*th-order *low-pass* transfer function approximation, that is, the numerator order is one less than denominator order.

M between 1 and 3 are valid. The Pade approximation is used.

If `[N,D]` are not given, the results are displayed.

Algorithm

`tfdelay` is an M-file in the *CSAD Toolbox*. Only standard MATLAB commands are used.

Purpose

Display the steady-state error constants and steady-state errors associated with an open-loop transfer function.

Synopsis

```
tfess
tfess(n,d)
```

Description

`tfess` computes the steady-state error constants and steady-state errors for a unit step, unit ramp, and $t^2/2$ parabolic system input associated with an open-loop transfer function. The user is prompted for the numerator and denominator of the transfer function.

`tfess(n,d)` uses n and d as the numerator and denominator, respectively.

Algorithm

`tfess` is an M-file in the *CSAD Toolbox*. It uses only standard MATLAB commands and other functions in the *CSAD Toolbox*.

Purpose

Find second order transfer function polynomials given a desired damping ratio ζ, and an undamped natural frequency ω_n.

Synopsis

```
tford2
tford2(zeta,Wn)
D=tford2
D=tford2(zeta,Wn)
[N,D]=tford2
[N,D]=tford2(zeta,Wn)
```

Description

`[N,D]=tford2` prompts the user for `zeta` and `Wn`, then returns `N` and `D` the numerator and denominator polynomial vectors, respectively.

`[N,D]=tford2(zeta,Wn)` uses the given `zeta` and `Wn`.

If only one output argument is used, the denominator vector `D` is returned.

If no output arguments are used, the results are displayed.

Algorithm

`tford2` is an M-file in the *CSAD Toolbox*. Only standard MATLAB commands are used.

See also

```
svord2
```

Purpose

To find the composite transfer function of two systems connected in parallel.

Synopsis

```
[N,D] = tfparall(Ng,Dg,K)
[N,D] = tfparall(Ng,Dg,Nh,Dh)
```

Description

`tfparall(Ng,Dg,Nh,Dh)` computes the composite transfer function $M(s) = G(s) + H(s)$ where `Ng` and `Dg` are the numerator and denominator of $G(s)$ and `Nh` and `Dh` are the numerator and denominator of $H(s)$.

`tfparall(Ng,Dg,K)` assumes that $H(s) = K$.

`N` and `D` are the numerator and denominator of $M(s)$, respectively. If `N` and `D` are not given, the results are displayed.

Algorithm

`tfparall` is an M-file in the *CSAD Toolbox*. It uses only standard MATLAB commands and other functions in the *CSAD Toolbox*.

See also

```
svparall, svcloop, svseries, tfcloop, tfseries
```

Purpose

To find the composite transfer function of two systems connected in series.

Synopsis

```
[N,D] = tfseries(Ng,Dg,K)
[N,D] = tfseries(Ng,Dg,Nh,Dh)
```

Description

tfseries(Ng,Dg,Nh,Dh) computes the composite transfer function $M(s) = G(s) \cdot H(s)$ where Ng and Dg are the numerator and denominator of $G(s)$ and Nh and Dh are the numerator and denominator of $H(s)$.

tfseries(Ng,Dg,K) assumes that $H(s) = K$.

N and D are the numerator and denominator of $M(s)$ respectively. If N and D are not given, the results are displayed.

Algorithm

tfseries is an M-file in the *CSAD Toolbox*. Only standard MATLAB commands are used.

See also

svparall, svcloop, svseries, tfcloop, tfparall

Purpose

To plot the unit step response of a system given its transfer function description.

Synopsis

```
tftplot
tftplot(N,D)
```

Description

tftplot computes and plots the unit step response of continuous-time systems represented by a transfer function.

tftplot prompts the user for the numerator and denominator polynomials, N and D, respectively, of the desired transfer function.

tftplot(N,D) uses N and D as the numerator and denominator polynomials, respectively.

The user interacts with tftplot by entering the *first letter* of the option desired when the following list is presented:

```
            – TFTPLOT OPTIONS –
        Plot          Final time
        Zoom in       New TF
        Set axes      Display TF
        Grid plot     Attributes
        Hold plot     Roots
        Label Plot    View data
                      Quit
```

The *first letter* is entered, and the return key is pressed. The action taken by each option is described as follows:

p   A plot of the unit step response is generated given the current N,D.
z   The user is asked to choose an area of the plot to enlarge by using a mouse or the keyboard. Plot grid and labels are lost.
s   The user is prompted for numerical values for the axis limits. The default response is to keep the present value.
g   A grid is drawn on the current plot.
h   Toggles the current state of hold. When hold is on, the future plots are

plotted on top of the current plot. When off, future plots appear on a new plotting surface.

l   Prompts the user for a title and *y*-axis label to place on the plot.

f   Prompts the user for a new final computation time.

n   Prompts the user for a new transfer function. Default entry is to keep the current transfer function.

d   Displays the current transfer function.

a   Computes and displays the attributes of the step response. The delay, rise, and settling times are computed as are the percent overshoot and time at the maximum.

r   Displays the zeros and poles of the current transfer function.

v   Prompts the user to identify a point on the current graph where the actual data is desired. The response and associated time of 15 points near the chosen point are displayed numerically.

q   Quits the function and returns control to the calling function or command screen.

There are six options not shown that also may be entered. They are

' '   (A space or a return key). Shows the current graph.

@   Prompts the user for text then places the text at a point on the current graph as instructed by the user.

Gets the coordinates of the graph pointed to by the user.

−   Prompts the user for the endpoints of a line, then plots a dotted line on the current graph.

^   Allows the user to set some of the parameters used within the function.

!   Passes the rest of the line entered to the function for evaluation and execution. All text following the exclamation point is evaluated. This command allows access to the internal variables of the function and allows the user to issue any MATLAB command. For example, `!meta` creates a graphics metafile of the current plot.

Algorithm

`tftplot` is an M-file in the *CSAD Toolbox*. It uses only standard MATLAB commands and other functions in the *CSAD Toolbox*. As with most numerical procedures, the accuracy of this function may deteriorate under a number of conditions. Keeping the order of the transfer function small (i.e., < 10) is helpful.

See also

`iltplot`

Purpose

Find a state transformation matrix that converts a system into controllable canonical form.

Synopsis

```
tr2ccf(A,B)
```

Description

tr2ccf returns the matrix **T** such that the system given by

$$\text{Abar} = \mathbf{T}^{-1}\mathbf{AT}, \quad \text{Bbar} = \mathbf{T}^{-1}\mathbf{B}, \quad \text{Cbar} = \mathbf{CT}, \quad \text{Dbar} = \mathbf{D}$$

is in controllable canonical form. **A**, **B** must be controllable for **T** to exist.

Algorithm

tr2ccf is an M-file in the *CSAD Toolbox*. Only standard MATLAB commands are used.

See also

```
sv2sv, tr2ocf, tr2df
```

Purpose

Find a state transformation matrix that converts a system into diagonal form.

Synopsis

```
tr2df(A)
```

Description

tr2df returns the matrix **T** such that the system given by

$$\text{Abar} = \text{T}^{-1}\text{AT}, \ \text{Bbar} = \text{T}^{-1}\text{B}, \ \text{Cbar} = \text{CT}, \ \text{Dbar} = \text{D}$$

is in diagonal form. **A** must have distinct eigenvectors for **T** to exist. This is guaranteed if **A** has distinct eigenvalues.

Algorithm

tr2df is an M-file in the *CSAD Toolbox*. Only standard MATLAB commands are used.

See also

```
sv2sv, tr2ccf, tr2ocf
```

Purpose

Find a state transformation matrix that converts a system into observable canonical form.

Synopsis

```
tr2ocf(A,C)
```

Description

`tf2ocf` returns the matrix **T** such that the system given by

$$\textbf{Abar} = \textbf{T}^{-1}\textbf{AT}, \ \textbf{Bbar} = \textbf{T}^{-1}\textbf{B}, \ \textbf{Cbar} = \textbf{CT}, \ \textbf{Dbar} = \textbf{D}$$

is in observable canonical form. **A**, **C** must be observable for **T** to exist.

Algorithm

`tr2ocf` is an M-file in the *CSAD Toolbox*. Only standard MATLAB commands are used.

See also

```
sv2sv, tr2ccf, tr2df
```

Index

The
MATH
WORKS
Inc.

Kuo

BUSINESS REPLY MAIL

FIRST CLASS   PERMIT NO. 82   NATICK, MA

POSTAGE WILL BE PAID BY ADDRESSEE

THE MATHWORKS, INC.
24 Prime Park Way
Natick, MA 01760-9889